The

Greatest

Basketball

Story

Ever Told

FOREWORD BY BOB HAMMEL

Greg Guffey

INDIANA

UNIVERSITY

PRESS

BLOOMINGTON · INDIANAPOLIS

The

THE

Greatest

MILAN

Basketball

MIRACLE,

Story

THEN AND

Ever Told

NOW

The paper used in this publication meets the minimum requirements of American National Standard for Information Sciences—Permanence of Paper for Printed Library Materials, ANSI Z39.48-1984.

Manufactured in the United States of America

Library of Congress Cataloging-in-Publication Data

Guffey, Greg.
    The greatest basketball story ever told : the Milan Miracle, then and now / Greg Guffey.
        p.   cm.
    ISBN 0-253-32688-5 (alk. paper). — ISBN 0-253-32689-3 (pbk. : alk. paper)
    1. Milan Indians (Basketball team)—History.   2. Basketball—Tournaments—Indiana—History.   I. Title.
GV885.42.M55G84   1993
796.323′62′09771′2—dc20   93-10366

   4 5 98

CONTENTS

To my parents, Jess and Connie Guffey

FOREWORD BY *Bob Hammel*

When John Gallman, director of Indiana University Press, told me that a young author had proposed doing a book on Milan's 1954 basketball team, I reacted with all the enthusiasm the fellow in the "I can't believe I ate the whole thing" commercial would have had for another pizza.

Not that I don't treasure that Milan story. I've always had a bit of trouble as a historian trying to put in proper order the biggest events of the fifties: Sputnik, the Korean War, *Brown v. the Board of Education*, the polio vaccine, Milan. Even in Indiana a vote for Milan as No. 1 seems a bit much, but . . .

Whatever Bill Clinton thinks to the contrary, it darned well beats Elvis.

But, gee, another piece on Milan is like another book on the Kennedy assassination. Can there possibly be an angle left?

Greg Guffey approached the subject with no angles, just the interest of a young journalist who grew up with basketball as a religious experience in New Castle, Indiana, and wondered about this thing that had happened long before he was born.

The movie *Hoosiers* probably contributed to his curiosity.

For me, that movie had been another experience in expected overkill and underappreciation. When the movie was being filmed and its theme became known, my instinct was protective and resentful. Hollywood could not possibly capture the Milan story. It could not possibly grasp how very good an entire state—with the exception of a major part of Muncie—could feel about itself and its passion, just because an appealing bunch of kids with a John R. Tunis–tailored coach had lived the impossible dream that Hoosiers had always held possible: that even a very small school could win the state high school basketball championship.

Now, Indiana is one of the few states where such an achievement would even be thought about, let alone possible. Most states don't even notice their annual high school tournament, and forty-seven of the fifty have multiple reasons for not notic-

ix

ing, because that many crown not a state champion but a diluting number of enrollment-class champions.

In Indiana, the theory always has been that if you're big enough to have five boys in your school, you can have a basketball team. And five is all the biggest school in the state can put on the floor at one time, so let's have at it.

Let us pause for some familiarization of terms for *Hoosiers* converts trying to grasp this phenomenon of Indiana tournament basketball.

Start with the levels of play. The tournament is spread over four weekends, similar to the NCAA, which shamelessly and admittedly copied—but not with the purity that Hoosiers prefer. Geography dictates everything in assignments in the Indiana tournament, and there is no seeding.

The first level of competition is the sectional, a gathering of neighbors that for the most part never changes. There are sixty-four of those, champions crowned on the last Saturday night in February or the first in March. They advance to sixteen regionals, where the one archaic part of the tournament comes into play, the one aspect that begs—for medical and logical reasons—to be corrected. That is the first of three straight tournament Saturdays on which teams, to advance, must win two games in one day. Games are played at 11:00 A.M. and about 1:00 P.M., and the winners meet at 8:15—for the second-game winner, five hours or less of recovery time.

The NCAA gives more mature athletes on college teams thirty-six hours between rounds, forty-eight or more at the Final Four. The Indiana High School Athletic Association, admirable in the main for its unbending adherence to rules ("The rules are clear and the penalty severe," one of its czars of the past said as a byword for sternness), stubbornly refuses to alter a format introduced when the game had the same thirty-two-minute time frame but was played with maybe half the trips up and down the court, when the clock kept going when the ball went out of bounds—and during the march from one end of the floor to midcourt for a center jump that followed every basket. One of the greatest Indiana high school stars ever, Rick Mount, had carried his 1966 Lebanon team seven-eighths of the way through the semistate elimination round before leg cramps stopped him and Logansport won. Feared is the day when a genuine tragedy is the result of such overexertion, but in Lebanon that sporting tragedy—so very avoidable with the application of common sense—never will be forgotten.

But, back to terminology: the winners from the sixteen regionals get together a Saturday later for the semistates. Until 1935 (the tournament started in 1911, twenty-eight years before the first NCAA tournament), the sixteen regional winners all advanced to the state tournament, where fifteen games had to be crammed into two days and the finalists were playing their fourth games in about thirty-six hours. Since '36, there have been semistates, which create the Final Four—a concept the NCAA didn't go to until 1952, and openly credited Indiana for the idea when it did.

"Final Four" is more of an NCAA term. In Indiana, the event when those select teams get together is called simply "the State." An Indiana high school championship is attained by winning the sectional, regional, semistate, and State, on consecutive Saturdays.

That's one glossary lesson to keep in mind, Hoosier basketball newcomer, while being a Guffey Reader.

Another is Hoosier pronunciation. This is not Italy; Milan is MY-lun, certainly not muh-LON. This is not France; Versailles is ver-SALES, not ver-SI. As Mark Twain wrote, foreigners always did spell better than they pronounce.

That's really about all the preparation you need to step into the past and relive, with its true characters, the actual *Hoosiers*—the phenomenon known simply as "The Miracle of Milan" for nearly forty years in Indiana now.

My initial fear that Hollywood would spoil a splendidly unspoiled story overlooked the loving and gentle care that was part of the project from the start, because its creators—scriptwriter Angelo Pizzo and director David Anspaugh—were Hoosiers whose basketball love and sensitivities motivated the whole thing. They deserve enormous credit, not just for their creativity but also for their will. They had the idea and the script long before they had a studio, and as young people in the business, they did need a film—for a start in their profession and for simple sustenance, artistic at least and not far from actual. One major studio offered to take it, with a few little alterations to make the whole thing more believable—like, a drug problem for this character, and . . .

Pizzo and Anspaugh walked out, and waited. And finally Orion Productions bought it as they had it, and it became a low-budget classic. Scene after scene from *Hoosiers* repeatedly is cited by athletes, teams, and coaches from across the country, not always in basketball. At the Barcelona Olympics, young U.S. runner Steve Holman said that he calmed his jitters before his first Olympic race by remembering what Coach Norman Dale in *Hoosiers* had done in pulling out a tape measure and showing that—even in huge, historic, lore-filled Butler Fieldhouse—the goals were just like home, ten feet high. All he had to do, Holman was saying, was run on a track that was just like home, 400 meters in length.

Others have cited the scene, just before the film's championship game, when a vow is made to win for all the small schools in the state—the scene when Jimmy Chitwood's shot is in the air and time stands still.

It was beautifully done, by two more artists who weren't old enough to see the Milan story happen and absorbed its wonder by osmosis. The film's greatness was recognized by several Oscar nominations, among them Pizzo for the screenwriting. Pizzo's devotion to basketball showed up on the night the Oscars were given that year: March 30, 1987. Pizzo had his tickets, his banquet table, his obvious dreams. But that night Indiana was playing Syracuse for the NCAA championship, and he stayed in his hotel room to watch and root. "In times of stress," he said later, "you go back to your roots."

The truth is, Mr. Pizzo and Mr. Anspaugh, though your story was wonderful, the real one was better. More dramatic. More schmaltzy. More gripping.

And, what young Greg Guffey had difficulty grasping, it also was more believable.

By the time Bobby Plump's basket delivered the state championship to Milan that March night in 1954, Indiana was unsurprised. It had been shocked that these kids from a school with just seventy-five boys had made it to "the State" the year before. When they returned, when they pounded a team with statewide respect, Indianapolis Attucks, in the semistate, and another, Terre Haute Gerstmeyer, in the first round at the State, theirs was no credibility problem. A generation or two later, Milan vs. Muncie Central for the championship seems a mismatch. It didn't then.

Milan won that game by numbers that seem flukish: 32–30. A slowdown. A freak winner. Milan had scored in the sixties in beating both Attucks and Gerstmeyer, and yes, that Attucks team did include the school's most famous—Indiana's most famous—basketball alumnus, Oscar Robertson, a sophomore then.

Milan could play—fast, or tactically slow. On the very floor where a legendary college coach, Tony Hinkle of Butler, taught a game that could batter equals and mousetrap more gifted teams, one of his students, Marvin Wood, proved his own coaching versatility and worth.

What Pizzo and Anspaugh, for all their sensitivity and skill, couldn't quite capture, what Greg Guffey, for all his research and perseverance, couldn't really grasp, is the feeling that Milan victory spread throughout the state—an afterglow that gave Hoosiers a benignly pleasant disposition for days and months, Hoosiers who had never been and never would get to Milan.

I've always considered it the best sports story ever, in a state blessed with so many.

And now it has been written one more time, with detail and insights from its primary players that I, a fair student in Milanology, had missed.

Happy reading, and remembering, and reminiscing.

ACKNOWLEDGMENTS

Like every book ever written, this one would not have been possible without the assistance of a number of people.

John Gallman, Director of Indiana University Press, took a chance when he agreed to do this book, and I am grateful to him for his belief in the project. The remainder of the staff at IU Press showed professionalism and courtesy when dealing with the editing, production, and marketing of the book. Bob Hammel, one of the best writers and one of the nicest men in the country, brought a fresh perspective and tireless editing to the manuscript. His work was invaluable.

Also near the top of this list is Jim Langford, Cub historian and director of the University of Notre Dame Press. He took an interest in this project when it was still an idea and helped many times along the way. His assistance is forever appreciated.

I must thank Dr. Barbara Allen and Dr. Ben Giamo in the American Studies Department at Notre Dame for their early belief in the worthiness of this project and for allowing me time to pursue it in my senior year. Thanks also go to John Powers, retired editor at the South Bend *Tribune* and journalism professor at Notre Dame, who was there in the beginning.

I am forever in debt to the Milan players, coaches, and townspeople. They allowed me to come into their homes, offices, and lives to tell their stories. I hope I have done those stories justice. I am also grateful to those who shared with me the photos from their personal collections. I don't want to cite a long list of names for fear of missing someone. Those people know who they are, and, to them, I say thanks.

Photographer Ron Tower, a lifetime friend, gave a lot of his time and effort to this book. So many other friends in New Castle, Notre Dame, and all over the great state of Indiana gave valuable insight, thoughtful advice, and lasting friendship along the way. For me, that's what it's all about.

The

Greatest

Basketball

Story

Ever Told

1 Introduction

Watch the tape and it seems difficult to believe. There's eighteen-year-old Robert Eugene Plump standing near midcourt, holding the ball, watching valuable seconds tick away in the championship game of the 1954 Indiana state basketball tournament. His team, tiny Milan from the southeast corner of the state, is *behind* in the final quarter, but Plump stands—the clock the only thing moving, action frozen at the hottest of all basketball times. The opposition, powerful Muncie Central, obliges and applies no pressure. For more than five minutes, Plump stands there. You want to reach through the television, back forty years in time, grab Plump, and shake him. "Do something, do anything, you're behind," you would say.

But all you can do is watch, as all those people in crammed Butler Fieldhouse did that night, and wait, as all those enraptured television watchers and radio listeners around the Hoosier state did. Five agonizing minutes later, Plump moved, Milan scored, and the game was tied. Then, just a few minutes later, the score still tied, he's there again. Only eighteen seconds remain, and in every mind there is a mental countdown—10 . . . 9 . . . 8 . . . 7 . . . This time, Plump has a chance to win the game, *the* game.

He shifts his weight one way, then another. He looks at the clock a couple of times, glances at the 30–30 score, but he just stands there—his four teammates spread to the far left side of the floor, their uncertain Muncie Central defenders right there with them.

Everyone knew what would happen next. First, Plump didn't want to shoot too soon and leave the Bearcats another chance to score. He knew everything there was to know about what he wanted, and needed, to do—except that a fictional character named Jimmy Chitwood would fire a similar shot thirty-two years later in a major motion picture, and a whole nation would cheer.

Eighteen seconds can be a lifetime when the future—of a town, a school, a twenty-six-year-old coach, and ten players—is on the line. All Plump had between himself and immortality was a quick Muncie Central defender named Jimmy Barnes. It would be Barnes who would ignominiously and undeservedly be forever linked with Plump, like baseball's Ralph Branca with Bobby Thomson. The other eight players were helpless, nonfactors. A lifetime of practice, a stellar high school career, four weeks of the state tournament, and more than thirty-one minutes against the most dominating Indiana high school basketball program ever had come down to one shot. Just one shot. Just you, the defender, the ball, and the basket. Make it, you're a folk hero for life. Miss it . . .

Plump was already in position to be the goat in these state finals. He was having his worst game of the entire tournament, just eight points in over thirty-one minutes. Maybe some were surprised that Milan coach Marvin Wood had put Plump in that climactic role, on this apparent off-night for him. How many chances can you give someone before it's time to try another plan?

But surely there weren't many thinking that. Plump was the horse Milan had ridden to the finals, and he would take them— win or lose—down the stretch. When he held the ball near midcourt, nothing else mattered. He could have had 2 points or 100 points. He could have been a rich city kid or the poor boy from the tiny Milan suburb of Pierceville that he actually was. For eighteen seconds, he had the attention of a state. Ever since, he has had its hearts.

Wood had called a time-out just seconds earlier to discuss the final play. The exact details of that discussion remain unclear. Four decades tend to cloud memories about specifics. Center Gene White says the decisive play happened exactly the way it was designed: guard Ray Craft was to inbound to Plump, who would wait until the final seconds to shoot. The others say that explanation is good enough for them.

"I don't remember thinking very much," Plump says. "I do remember asking to go over it again."

Plump evidently had a short memory, because *he* took the ball out of bounds. Craft quickly tossed it back to him to set up the final play. It was one-on-one, as he had played for his entire young basketball life. No one asked for anything fancy, just score one basket, against one defender.

"Once I get the ball, things just disappear," Plump says. "I don't remember the fans. I don't remember anybody except one man, and that was Jimmy Barnes. It was the same thing as playing in the backyard. All I had to do was beat him. How many times had I done that before?"

"We knew what was going to happen and did everything we could to stop it," said Muncie Central coach Jay McCreary after the game. "If I'd had a rifle, I'd have shot that ball right out of the sky and let them argue for the next ten years about whether or not it would have gone in. But I didn't have any rifle."

Plump eyed Barnes, faked left once, dribbled to his right, shot, and hit. Muncie Central had no time to get a final shot.

Today, Plump leans back in his chair and looks toward the ceiling. He is far from cocky, not the kind to hit a shot and then shake his fist in an opponent's face. Friends, even casual acquaintances, call him one of the nicest people they have ever met. That doesn't mean he ever lacked self-confidence. With a gaze toward the ceiling that takes him back forty years, he insists quietly, "I knew when I let it go that it was going in."

• • •

Ray Craft, Milan's other starting guard, didn't really know what to do after Plump hit that last-second shot. "My biggest feeling was that a big weight had been lifted and we had finally won it," Craft said. "It was a great relief. The tournament was over and we had won."

No one could have realized the magnitude of what had happened. Tiny Milan had edged huge Muncie Central 32–30 before a sold-out Butler Fieldhouse crowd in the capital city of Indianapolis. How can any eighteen-year-old look past the moment and into the future, knowing the consequences that thirty-two minutes of basketball would have on a team, a town, and a state? Wasn't it just another game, like the ones they played as kids with the old goal nailed on reserve guard Roger Schroder's family store in Pierceville, a town with a population of about fifty which turned out four of those state champion players?

No, it wasn't. It was much more than just another game in a state tourney with a history of "games of the century." That one night changed basketball forever in a state where players are gods and winter weekend nights are heaven. "The Milan Game" is still the measuring stick for great games, and few others have made a serious challenge.

"I'm glad people still talk about it," Plump said. "You're talking about the formative years of your life, maybe when you had more fun than at any other time. Not many people get an opportunity to still do that. There have been a lot of memorable experiences since then, but I don't think that in the fifties there was anything from an athletic standpoint to give an individual more instantaneous thrills and a greater sense of accomplishment than winning the state tourney."

This is Indiana basketball: forty years later people still argue over who really had the better team that season. Was it a once-in-a-lifetime lucky shot, or did Milan actually have the better squad? Muncie Central coach Jay McCreary, now retired and living in Louisiana, says the years haven't clouded his vision about that state tournament.

"I really felt we had the best ballclub," says McCreary, who won the state title with Muncie Central in 1952. "We had guys who could play basketball. Milan wasn't just a run-of-the-mill ballclub either. But we had the best ballclub. We just didn't prove we had the best ballclub. There's a big difference. Anybody can beat anybody on a given night. That's what makes sports great."

As Milan celebrated on the court, McCreary and his Bearcats

headed to the locker room. They couldn't believe they had actually lost the game. They were the great Muncie Central Bearcats, the invincible team, the one that had won more state titles than most Milan players had watched. The Muncie Central Bearcats were winning state titles before the Milan Indians ever won a sectional. Somewhere, somehow, something went wrong.

McCreary remembers players sitting for almost an hour in that basement locker room, not even removing their jerseys. "We had seniors in that locker room who said they couldn't even take the jersey off because they would never put it on again. That's how much it meant to the kids, to be there and lose in the state championship."

Upstairs in the arena, Pat Stark, an Indianapolis policeman, ran across the court through the jubilant crowd and stormed down a tunnel into the Milan locker room. He had escorted Milan for the past two years during their Indianapolis trips, and the Indian players liked him so much they had actually pried him away from another assigned team in the 1954 semistate. Now this team that had absorbed him into its midst was a winner. *His* winner. It was his turn to celebrate with the state champions.

"By God, tonight's my night," he shouted at the half-amazed and half-scared players. "I'm going to do it. I don't care what happens. You've made my dream come true."

Former Milan player Bob Engel recalls, "He threw his hat in the air and grabbed hold of a player. He just kept saying, 'I'm going to do it. I'm going to do it.' "

What Stark did was escort the most improbable championship team on the most unlikely championship celebration ever. Violating all department regulations, he set his lights to flashing, activated his siren, and led a tiny procession of player-carrying Cadillacs from Butler Fieldhouse almost five miles through the Indianapolis streets to the heart of the city—a block-wide, circular street that encloses a towering monument. It's a one-way street. On this special night, Stark led the parade of Cadillacs the wrong way around the circle. The stunt bottlenecked traffic, and startled drivers honked. The parade went around and around and around—three times. "The chief called me in and chewed me out," Stark told Engel years later. "I wouldn't have cared if he had fired me."

This was the Miracle of Milan. This was Milan High School,

with just seventy-five boys in the upper four grades. This was Milan, a town of 1,100 in a remote corner of the state. Most of these people knew Indianapolis only through newspapers, but they owned the place for one night. They owned the whole state. Rare is a Hoosier over fifty who says he or she didn't watch or listen to that game when Plump hit that last-second jumper and David slew Goliath.

They deserved that ride around Monument Circle. Someone should have opened the gates to the Indianapolis Motor Speedway and let the winners take a real victory lap. That wrong-way trip around downtown was the mid stage of the biggest celebration in the history of basketball anywhere. "I don't think anyone has had a celebration like that since," says starting center Gene White. "We just thought that was the way it was supposed to be."

When the players and coaches arrived back in Milan the next afternoon—still escorted by Stark—a crowd estimated at more than 20,000 greeted them. This wasn't for a president, or even the governor or a military hero. This was for a high school basketball team, a group of fifteen-to-eighteen-year-olds who had no idea of the impact they would eventually have on basketball everywhere as long as the game is played. This was for a group of teenagers who thought a big night on the town meant hanging out at the local restaurant. This was for a group who never had much, but they had basketball, so what else really mattered?

It wasn't that this team didn't deserve such a celebration. Take every upset in the world of sports, add them together, and in Indiana they still wouldn't equal what Milan did all those years ago. Few, very few, people gave Milan much of a chance that night. After all, it was a school of 160 playing a school of 1,200. Bush league against big league. This game was supposed to show once and for all that Indiana needed to bring its tournament up to date and develop a system of competition where teams played against opponents of similar enrollments.

Instead, Milan's victory ended that thinking. Maybe forever. All tournaments have upsets. This one, more than thirty years later, was the basis for a nationally popular movie, *Hoosiers.*

"I still think that if we had won the ballgame, the tournament would have gone to classification," McCreary says. In the next breath, McCreary says it one more time: He had the better team.

Maybe.

Maybe not.

It's not as simple as McCreary would have people believe. Milan didn't leap out of the woodwork in that state tourney and win a championship. The Indians had advanced to the Final Four in 1953 before losing to eventual state champion South Bend Central in the afternoon semifinal. They had returned three-fifths of their lineup. They had the experience of having been there, and sometimes that means more than tradition. Muncie Central was good, but not great. The Bearcats, losers of five games during the regular season, had proven they were not invincible. They were definitely favored, but the debate will always remain open over whether they were actually better.

Not arguable is that almost two generations later, Indiana still has a one-class tournament, and Bobby Plump is a folk hero, the kind that people call from bars at two in the morning to see if he really did hit that shot forty years ago or if the drunk next to them has had one too many. And he's also the kind of hero who still keeps his telephone number listed and who actually doesn't mind when someone makes that call.

It made the tiny town of Milan a haven for basketball purists. It made those ten players and their coaches icons. It also created a link that blurred the boundaries between the past and the present as the town and players tried to deal with the miracle that happened way back in 1954.

This is a story of a team and a town, much like the ones in *Hoosiers* but real—and their story is better. It's a story of growing old and hanging on. And one of refusing to let go because what the Milan Indians did on that March night in '54 forever changed people and places.

2 *The Town*

The water tower, the one with "State Champs 1954" painted across it, serves as a daily reminder for Milan residents of that historic night. But it's not like a reminder is needed. How can you forget the greatest game in the history of the Indiana state high school basketball tourney, maybe the greatest game in basketball history? That rusting, fading water tower symbolizes the best moment the town of 1,100 has ever seen—the best time Milan will ever see.

"If you go over to Nineveh [pop. 1,500], they'll talk about a team that got in the final game of the sectional," says Gene White, the starting center for the '54 champions. "That's typical of the small town. The best basketball team they ever had will be the yardstick for schools that aren't even in that town anymore. People don't understand the degree to which a small town gets enthused about it. In our era, basketball was the dominant thing. Basketball was the sport. Every town had a gym and every town had a team. It was a poor man's game."

That made it the right game for Milan. People were poor but no

8

one knew it, because every family was in the same economic situation. The ten players who dressed for that 1954 tournament rarely ventured outside Milan unless the trip involved basketball. They had nothing but each other and really expected nothing more. But they were happy because they had family, friends, and, maybe most of all, basketball. Four—Bobby Plump, Gene White, Roger Schroder, and Glenn Butte—came from Pierceville, a town that truly met the Indiana definition of tiny. It didn't have a high school or a basketball team. It sent its students three miles south into the Milan school system. The remaining six—Ray Craft, Bob Engel, Ron Truitt, Ken Wendelman, Rollin Cutter, and Bill Jordan—grew up in Milan.

They remember playing together as long as they remember playing at all. They tell a lot of stories. They tell of most growing closer and some growing apart, of beating the high school team during lunch when they were just eighth-graders, of how probably none would have gone to college if not for basketball. They tell how much they love Milan and how sad they feel watching the town die a slow death. They tell of making basketball their lives and achieving a dream. As they grow older, the stories grow taller and bolder. That happens when you become legends.

Today, a small green sign hangs under Milan's town marker, boasting of former resident Jenny Johnson, "world's first lady of softball." The small diamond north of the school is named in her honor. Johnson, like seemingly everyone else who has achieved success in Milan, has long since moved on. She is the women's athletic director at Franklin College. But make no mistake about it, softball will never compare with basketball in Milan. Basketball—roundball, as Engel calls it—is the game. Always has been. Always will be. It's not the nineties version that excites people—at least not with a Milan team that was 0–20 in 1990–91 and won just one game a year later—but the 1954 Team of History. It was the championship season, the one that the old-timers still relive, the one that they may have relived once too often.

Father Time, the saying goes, waits for no one, not even the town that produced the team that beat Muncie Central. According to the Milan residents, the producers of *Hoosiers* said the town was too commercialized to use in filming. Where they looked, no one knows. A Dairy Queen on Indiana 101 is the only sign that the sixties ever came to Milan, let alone the seventies, eighties, and nineties. The relatively low-budget movie became a surprise national success, and it also drew surprising resentment and anger from many of the Milan players and townspeople. "Go down the main street of Milan; if that's not the fifties or earlier, I don't know what is," says Butte, who called the movie "pure Hollywood."

There have been many great Indiana high school teams over the years—Franklin's Wonder Five in the early 1920s, Oscar Robertson's Indianapolis Crispus Attucks teams in the fifties, Marion's three straight state champions in the eighties. Milan's '54 squad probably wouldn't make a lot of all-time Top Tens. The team wasn't flashy. There was no real superstar, though Plump in his day was close. They dared to put crowds to sleep with their occasional cat-and-mouse style of play, and even in their glory year, they weren't even in the polls' Top Fifteen when the state tourney began. And only one player, Plump, made an impact on the collegiate level.

But they won the biggest of the big games, and the way they won that final game—small-time over big-time, the last-second shot, the Cinderella story—assured them of their place in history. They were, and still are, the smallest school since Thorntown in 1915 to win the state. The uniqueness didn't really take hold until later, because the odds were that some other small school *could* duplicate Milan's large feat. No team has matched it in forty seasons. Some have come close, but who remembers those invited to the dance who wind up watching the others tango? In fact, the smallest school to make it to the Final Four in the last forty years other than Milan in '54 is Milan in '53. The fact that the '53 team had such success hints that maybe, just maybe, against the beliefs and rallying cries of Muncie Central coach Jay McCreary, the win in '54 wasn't such an upset.

"That's the game everybody still talks about," says Bob Williams, who covered the game for the Indianapolis *Star* and is now sports information director for the Indiana High School Athletic Association (IHSAA). "It's had a big impact. We've had a lot of small schools come to the Final Four since then. Nobody has been able to do what Milan did in 1954. The fact that it was a small school and they were playing the biggest basketball power in the state made it even better. We've had a lot of great games, but that's the one remembered by most people as the biggest and most exciting game."

Nineteen fifty-four, now that was the season. Some will say that time began and ended in Milan with that season. The championship provided a one-way ticket out for the players, and a lifetime of memories for the town. It gave that small town an identity, but it also created a time warp which still exists today. "I still have to realize that time changes everything," says 1954 coach Marvin Wood. "It has changed me. It has changed the community. It has changed the young men who played for us while we were there."

Indeed, the lives of those ten players who dressed for that '54 tourney changed forever. They were heroes instead of small-town high school boys. Their stories are similar, yet unique. They were united by both school and a dream. They grew apart but at the same time grew much closer.

The town remains locked in the fifties as the twenty-first century approaches. The prospects are grim for revival, but when you've had the greatest moment in the greatest game in the greatest sport the state has ever known, does anything else really matter? It was James Naismith, the father of basketball, who once visited Indiana and said, "The possibilities here are endless." Did he know? Could anybody have known?

Early in the movie version of this fabled story, Barbara Hershey says to Gene Hackman, "A basketball hero around here is treated like a god. How can he ever find out what he can really do? I don't want this to be the high point of his life. I've seen them, the real sad ones. They sit around the rest of their lives talking about the glory days when they were seventeen years old."

"Most people," replies Hackman, "would kill to be treated like a god just for a few moments."

The players on this team have been treated like gods for four decades now, but they are not the sad ones reliving those glory days. Most love to talk about them, but they have also moved on to better things. Theirs are stories worth handing down to future generations. The town has seen better days, but it too has a story, a tale of a love affair with a basketball team in a time when basketball meant everything. The tale still lives today.

• • •

Milan is a one-caution-light town located in the gentle hills of southeastern Indiana, thirty-six miles from Cincinnati and seventy-four miles from Indianapolis. State Road 101 winds from the east through Sunman, a no-caution-light town that also has fallen on hard times. The road dead-ends once, leaving two dirt-road options to nowhere and a paved highway to Milan. An old metal basketball goal with no net on the outskirts of town gives the only indication that hoops is what this town is all about.

A large rectangular board greets visitors just after that small town marker. In the upper right corner is a large basketball logo with "1954 STATE CHAMPS" printed within it. There are other logos on the board, the kind Lions Clubs and similar small-town organizations feel obligated to have, but nothing is as large as that basketball. It is this town's undying symbol.

One might expect too much upon entering Milan, with that paved road and modern million-dollar high school just inside the city limits. The JayC store next to the school may not be Kroger's, but it will suffice. The Dairy Queen on the right is the kind with walk-up service only. A cluster of businesses—a plumbing supply store, a thrift shop, and another grocery—sit opposite the Dairy Queen. That thrift shop was once the Milan Drugstore until the owner dropped pharmaceuticals. Instead of making a new sign, he simply chiseled the "drug" out of "drugstore" and it became the Milan Store. Dorothy Sullender lives in the Milan Lamplite Villa, a small independent-living retirement community directly behind the small grocery. Formerly Dorothy Plump, she virtually raised brother Bob after their mother died when he was just five years old.

A left turn in the opposite direction of the main drag leads to the million-dollar elementary school and the parking lot where the old gymnasium once sat. That's where the '53 Indians played their home games before administrators moved the team to the larger and newer gym twelve miles south in Versailles for the '54 home games. The town hall and the power plant are next to that parking lot flanked by Lakeside Country Club, across the railroad tracks.

The area's closest brush with luxury, Lakeside offers nine holes of golf on a simple yet beautiful course given sparkle by a majestic lake that no one ever bothered to name. Eat lunch in the small but comfortable clubhouse, look out at the course, and wonder what a jewel like this is doing in a place like Milan. Members come from all around the southeastern Indiana area, with annual dues less than a third the cost of competing clubs. Owners recently purchased fifty acres of land adjacent to the club, with plans to enlarge the course to eighteen holes.

There's a Shell station just across the railroad tracks on Highway 101. A television and appliance store south of the gas station is followed by a liquor store. Houses line the opposite side of the highway. A quick right turn onto Carr Street, once the main drag to end all main drags, quells any optimism about economic revival.

Milan's main downtown street is one-way and straight out of the fifties, except that many of the buildings that bustled then are vacant now. The progress known as interstates, bypasses, and suburbs has done wonders for Cincinnati and other larger cities, but it has drained the life out of Milan. A drive down Carr Street gives the sense of a small town down on its luck, but even that doesn't tell the real story. In the heyday of the fifties, Carr Street had twenty businesses on the north side of the street and sixteen on the south side; now there are just over a dozen total.

The north side offered a barbershop, Rosie Arkenberg's restaurant, Richmond Jewelry, Chris Volz's garage, Kroger's grocery, another barbershop, the post office, a dress shop, a liquor store, a tailor shop, the corner drugstore, a license branch, a general store, a beauty shop, the General Electric store, another dress shop, a lumber yard, a feed mill, a furniture factory, and the Chevrolet garage. The south side had the King Hotel, a meat market, the JayC store, a gas station, Silverman's Plumbing, a bookstore, Krick's Electric, Kirschner's Hardware, Krick Bottle Gas, a show building, a bank, a third barbershop, the Tot Shop, a shoe store, an insurance company, a tool and die store, and a hospital.

The Railroad Inn, built in 1980, features dining, four hotel rooms, and an apartment. It, like every other business, is linked with the past. Pictures from the 1954 season line the entrance, and a glass case displays the letter jacket of Gene White, the starting center for the champions.

The street dead-ends near that water tower, an appropriate place because that is also when and where time ended. The old tower is neglected now, rusting, peeling, living out its days. Weeds grow around it, and water accumulates after a long rain.

It is one of three towers in a town with major water problems, but its productive days are over. No one comes out here anymore. They remember; they just don't pay too many visits. The town still owns the land and even placed some "no trespassing" signs in the vicinity.

Some of the buildings on that main street are gone, some are apartments, some sit empty. None of the buildings, with the possible exception of the barbershop, are comparable to the way they were in the fifties. Thompson Furniture Company, once the town's largest employer at about 150 people, went out of business and sold the huge building next to the railroad tracks to Dolly Madison, which lasted there just a few years before declaring bankruptcy. Local lore has it that the building sat idle for several years until the owners took out an insurance policy, then it burned to the ground a few weeks later.

A couple of blocks from the Railroad Inn is Baker Chevrolet, an auto dealership started decades ago by Milan legend Chris Volz. It was Volz who, in both '53 and '54, provided shiny new cars to carry the team to its tournaments—different cars for each stage of the tournament. The Milan players went to the regional in Pontiacs, the semistate in Buicks, and the state in Cadillacs. For that one imaginative act that was part of the team's lore, Chris Volz had statewide identity for two generations.

Chester Nichols, owner of Nichols Barbershop, is the last of a breed. He has cut hair in that same shop since 1950; his father started the business in 1932. In the last forty years, Nichols has seen the downtown area die a little bit at a time. His is the only downtown business that has survived intact since 1950.

Nichols has a two-chair shop, the kind Floyd Lawson always wanted on the Andy Griffith show. His shop was once the true-life version of the shop in *Hoosiers*—the focal point of downtown when he had two chairs, three always-busy barbers, and a standing-room crowd of men who would come in, sit, and talk or argue or listen for hours. He's lucky now if a few come in to just have their hair cut. He charges $4.50 for a haircut and $1.00 for a shave. A shave? In the nineties?

Nichols talks freely about the good days, when downtown was still alive and a shave and haircut were still in vogue. He sits back in his chair, tilts his head toward the ceiling, and thinks for a few seconds before answering any questions. He is blunt, and maybe

14

he exaggerates at times. He has just finished one haircut; another customer sits in the long row of chairs just passing time and shooting the breeze.

"We've lost over a hundred business places," Nichols says. "When the Milan Hospital left, they took better than 50 percent of the businesses with them. Back in the fifties, we had businesses in here, all kinds of businesses. We had one of the best Kroger stores around until it moved to Aurora. Every building in this street had a business in it. It's been a heck of a change. Any time you lose a business out of a town, it hurts. We used to open at six in the morning and work until twelve at night."

He wouldn't even guess how many haircuts that was.

"You didn't count them; you just did it. Back then, you would give more shaves than haircuts. Over here [he points over his shoulder] we had five racks of mugs for shaves. Everybody in town had their own mug. We would give ten shaves to maybe every one haircut. I only give about three a week now. Nobody has time."

Habits have changed but not the people—at least not in the mind of Chet Nichols.

"From my point of view, the people in the town of Milan are wonderful. But we had 1,000 people in 1940 and we had 1,277 forty years later. That shows you how much we grew. I'm not trying to be sarcastic. I'm just telling it like it is. We've had a lot of people move in. When they come in, I'll ask them where they live and they'll give me some road number that doesn't mean a thing to me. I'll say, 'Who is your next-door neighbor?' and they don't even know. It used to be you'd say, 'Go to the big oak tree and go so many houses' to where somebody lived. I recently told somebody where a guy lived, and he went by the road three or four times and came back and said there wasn't anybody out there. He's probably still out there looking for him. Used to be, you went by rocks, you went by trees, you went by properties. In the city, you had to go by street signs. Out here, you didn't."

There are other businesses in the Milan school district. The only problem is that few of them employ more than a handful of people. This is just a trace of what used to be and a sad result of what might have been. "Our town," says longtime high school secretary Betty Dobson, "is basically a ghost town. We have not progressed too much. We've got more vacant buildings than we

15

have open ones." Other businesses are spread out over town—cleaners, gas stations, garages, the meat market—but not enough to make much of a difference. There are also churches, lots of them: Baptist, Methodist, Catholic. Name a denomination and it will probably be here.

In the late forties and early fifties, Milan was like any other small town in rural America. Arkenberg's Restaurant was the local hangout, closing during games and reopening to serve fans afterwards until two in the morning. People, the oldtimers say, waited for hours to get a seat and rehash the games. The informal Downtown Coaches Club, which met daily to second-guess Marvin Wood and critique the players, had a regular table there. The players had a meal allowance after every game. After that championship game, a sign in the window read, "We took it all but the capital and Mr. Craig" (George, Indiana governor at the time).

When Milan won the title, there were profits in everything. Photographer William McGhee rented a small section of the corner drugstore and did what the Louisville *Courier-Journal* called "a land office business selling pictures of the team and the championship game." When the small Milan Shoe Store closed so its owners could attend the big game, a sign on the front of the store read, "Moccasin trading post closed 10 A.M. Saturday—Warrior, squaw and papoose gone to great pow-wow."

It was, to put it bluntly, a good time, the *best* time, for Milan.

If Milan is a ghost town, even-smaller Pierceville is barely a spot on the map anymore. It, too, has succumbed to progress. The most impressive site in the area is the Seagrams warehouse halfway between Milan and Pierceville on Highway 350. Coach Wood worked there in the summer of '53. But the warehouse is not a factory and employs just another handful of people.

A large dump, with what look to be remnants of a once-proud town, greets visitors at the edge of Pierceville. Tractors, cars, furniture, food, clothing—they're all there. A service station sits abandoned just beyond the dump, with tall weeds growing around the cement blocks that once held the gas pumps. A left turn across the railroad tracks onto County Road 750 leads into the heart of Pierceville, what's left of it.

Roger Schroder grew up in the house on the corner just across the tracks, and his family operated the general store adjacent to the house. That store is perhaps the saddest victim of all this

16

decay, with every window covered by different kinds and colors of boards. No sign hangs at the back of the building to boast that four of the champions once perfected their game here. Grass has grown over the playing court. Who knows what happened to the goal.

Today, it looks like the discarded buildings in every small, decaying town in every part of America. Maybe—surely—someone could at least put a marker there, like those at the graveyard, to tell that the most hallowed champions in Hoosier history once lived and ate and laughed and played here.

The building along the railroad tracks that served as White's Feed Store was vacated long ago. Grass and weeds cover the structure, just a shadow of its former self. The new owners moved Schroders' store into a building about a hundred yards onto State Road 350. Patrons still must manually reset the gas pumps.

Some of Pierceville's few roads have never been paved and probably never will be. The houses, many big, most old, and all showing signs of their age, are the kind with chairs on the front porch where people actually sit and read the evening paper— where in the summertime, with a big pitcher of sun tea, they talk about the golden days when the town was alive and a farming community was in the present tense, not the past. The houses definitely have seen better days. Many qualify as shacks. Tractors, cars, toys sit in the front yards. Pierceville still is a God-fearing place like most other small towns in Indiana, and the residents in the main gather to hear the gospel at the United Methodist Church behind Schroders' old store every Sunday morning.

The fifties were definitely different. People talked about prosperity instead of dreaming about it. And basketball was the center of attention, the only thing. If you didn't like basketball, then you probably didn't expect to have many friends or social events from October to April. "Basketball, there was nothing else," said Dobson. "Everybody ate, drank, and slept basketball." Wood said of that Milan: "Basketball was on the tips of everybody's tongues. Basketball was the most important thing in that part of the state. Everyplace you went, people wanted to talk basketball."

Plump called it "about the most important thing there was. It was the focal point of all the attention. For the people of Milan, it was something that drew them together. It was something they could be extremely proud of. It was bragging rights in the county if you were good. It created rivalries. When you had 1,000 season ticket holders for 1,000 seats, there had to be some interest."

A week after the basketball team won at Butler Fieldhouse, twenty-five local businesses bought a full-page advertisement in the Versailles *Republican*. It read in part, "Your achievement in the Indiana tournament in 1954 will remain in our hearts forever. Your hard work and determination has brought fame and glory to our community and county that will be remembered in Indiana high school basketball as long as this sport is played. You have proven what teamwork can do. When ten boys really cooperate with each other they can bring home the championship." Of those twenty-four advertisers, only two firms—Chris Volz Motors, now owned by Daren Baker, and Red Smith Insurance Agency, also under a different owner—remain in business.

The overriding thought, and the one many prefer to avoid, is what might have been had progress made a stop in Milan along with the thousands of sightseers who came in the wake of the 1954 miracle. Founded in 1854, exactly one hundred years before that fateful season, Milan was a farming and small business community linked to both small and large cities by the Baltimore and Ohio Railroad, which still runs through the center of town. That same railroad ran through Pierceville some three miles north, bringing business and prosperity to that area as well.

The Mishawaga Springs Hotel, a luxurious spa and recreation center that boasted pure mineral water, a golf course, riding stables, and a ten-acre lake, was the area's top attraction. Local lore has it that the hotel also attracted many of the area's biggest gamblers. The prosperity didn't last for long; the hotel burned to the ground in 1927, and the owners never rebuilt. Hindsight might now see that as the beginning of the end.

Some say Milan had outstanding prospects for growth after that 1954 season. Several companies wanted to build small factories in the area, attracted in part by the town's magic name, but land owners refused to sell. "I think what really has hurt me is the growth that the town could have had," Engel said. "There were four or five key people who kept it from expanding, and they're gone now. They lingered too long on that year. They hung on too long."

So, other towns jumped at the chance for prosperity. Lawrenceburg had lured Seagrams. Columbus now has Arvin Industries. Madison has Cummins Diesel. An atomic energy plant is in nearby Hamilton, Ohio. Seymour has a huge Walmart Distribution Center. Milan residents commute to jobs outside the town rather than finding work within it.

"Milan seems to me like it is dying," says Ray Craft. "It disappoints me to drive through town and see what I thought were real nice homes that are deteriorating. Milan looks like a town that is not going to prosper. There are some nice homes left, but the downtown area is just about gone. There would have to be a reason to move into Milan. I really don't know of anything in Milan to attract business to make it flourish again."

The pride is still there, because something great happened in 1954. Drive through many similar towns in southern Indiana and try to find that pride. There is resentment, bitterness, and talk about big cities and suburbs killing their way of life. No regrets hang over Milan. That title was so great because it was won by ten boys who had only the expectations of becoming the next generation of farmers. It was a community of people helping people, mainly because no one knew any differently. It was their way of life. "They'd say, 'Hey, it's wintertime and a kid needs a new coat,' " said Betty Dobson. "They would put a can down at the drugstore or under the counter somewhere and the kid would get his new coat. Anybody that needed help got help."

"It's hard for people to realize that back in the fifties you didn't have much, but I think you had a lot more closeness," said Engel. "It wasn't just families but communities. I can't say enough about the people. They say, 'You put us on the map.' I say, 'Sure, but look at the sacrifices you made for us.' A lot of people didn't have a kid on the team but they were there for you."

The people of Milan, at least those around in 1954, are still friendly, almost too friendly. An old commercial recalled a time when a handshake and a man's word meant something. That's still true here. They never lock the doors to their houses, and they never see a strange face. They are protected by a police staff of just one marshal and his deputy, yet the oldtimers can't remember the last shooting or any other major crime activities. "One time," says longtime assistant coach Marc Combs, "a couple of guys had too many drinks down at the tavern and got in a

19

little fistfight." It is a slice of simple America in a time of national complexity, and the residents would have it no other way. "We're always going to be a quiet, sleepy town," says Baker, owner of that local GM dealership, the largest full-line dealer within several miles. "That's all we can really expect."

What will also never change is that thousands of people, most since the release of *Hoosiers,* have made this tiny spot on the map a stop on their vacations. One couple from Kansas City saw the movie twenty-seven times before deciding it was time to see the real thing. Another couple called Craft, now the assistant commissioner of the IHSAA, and said they were having trouble finding Hickory on an Indiana state map. He then explained that Hickory was just a fictional school in the movie. So the couple visited Milan instead.

The problem is that there isn't a lot to see. A trip to the new school and gym, one of the most modern in the state, is a must. The main entrance to the school has a two-part trophy case under a computer banner that reads, "Math is the right one baby, uh-huh." That case holds the two commemorative basketballs from the sectional champions of the eighties—the 1980 team and the 1985 team that Gene White coached. The real memorabilia, the prizes from '54, have their special place in the gymnasium. A huge frame featuring individual 8 x 10 photos of all ten players along with Wood and Combs hangs above another trophy case at the west entrance of the gym. The state championship trophy, along with other trinkets accumulated over the years, sits majestically in the middle of the trophy case below that frame. Three banners—from the championship season, the '53 Final Four trip, and a semistate advancement in '73—along with large accompanying team photos hang on the west end inside the 1,800-seat gym.

Tourists still literally come by the busloads to Milan. Rosslyn McKittrick, former owner of the Railroad Inn, moved to the town after that 1954 season. Once she greeted each bus outside the restaurant. She would get on the bus with a Cincinnati Reds hat, switch to an Indiana Hoosier hat, and finally don her Milan cap. "There wasn't a person on those buses that hadn't heard of Milan, Indiana," she said. Now McKittrick owns an antique store where she sells, among other things, newspaper reprints from the season, championship paperweights, and recordings of the final game.

Milan has managed to maintain its identity through refusals to consolidate with other school corporations, yet this pride has weakened the school's athletic programs. Of the twenty-eight teams that played Milan in 1954, eleven no longer exist, swallowed in mergers. As other schools have grown and diversified their enrollment bases, Milan has remained relatively constant. There are more students enrolled at the school, but that unwillingness to consolidate hindered what it was supposed to preserve: school pride, athletic pride, basketball pride. So be it: sentimentality means something, means everything, to the small communities. "It's still Milan, and it's the same area that has been covered since that game," McKittrick said. "Keeping our schools with the name Milan has kept our identity. It's been a stepping stone because everyone recognizes the name Milan."

A look at the current state of the basketball program shows the results of that refusal to consolidate: a winless season in 1990–91, only a single victory the following year, and then just two in the 1992–93 season under a new head coach. And the future prospects for Milan are not exactly bright.

"I saw feast and famine," says Glenn Butte, now the athletic director in nearby Batesville. "That was difficult to take, and it was difficult for the people in town to take. The prospects of winning in the future don't look good. It's hard for the people in Milan, and it's hard for me when you look back. What's happening now is that the basketball talent is at a low ebb. It's difficult to get out of that. No one wants their identity closed. It's part of the religion in Indiana that you want your names on that jersey on the basketball uniform. They weren't going to go together with anybody and lose their identity after having that glorious championship."

Says Engel, "They just wouldn't commit themselves to consolidation. I'm sure as I'm sitting here that there would have been a different atmosphere in that town. You could have had more people, a bigger community. The people on the school board at that time, all they lived for was basketball, to think that we might get back to the big barn again." The "big barn." Butler Fieldhouse. The state finals.

All ten of the boys who dressed for that championship game

used basketball as a way out of Milan to better things. Craft and White returned for brief coaching stints, and Wendelman lives a short trip south in the county seat of Versailles. The rest never came back. They went to Michigan, Texas, California, and all over Indiana, but they never permanently came back to their hometown. Over the subsequent post-championship years, young people saw Milan as a stopping place on the way to higher achievements, unthinkable before college education became a necessity rather than an exception. In a day when high school graduates usually went to work in the family business, nine of those ten players attended college. That statistic was in stark contrast to the fact that just one member of the entire class of 1938, just sixteen years earlier, left the hometown of Milan after graduation.

During his return to Milan as the basketball coach, White tried unsuccessfully to revive the town. "I don't think you'd ever see it grow into a metropolis," he said. "We tried various things to lure a business when I was on the town board. Milan is on a railroad, near an interstate. A business could relocate there. But we never found one."

McKittrick has taken over that search for new businesses. She cites statistics that more than a hundred businesses currently operate in the Milan school district, but the problem is that most cannot provide the jobs and pump the money into the local coffers to help rebuild. Milan needs some kind of economic miracle: a major manufacturer moving in.

But maybe that one miracle, in 1954, is all this town can really expect. "I don't know what could top it," Baker says. Milan is content in knowing that it had one big moment, one moment when time stopped and it was the focus of an entire state. Most other small, dying towns have failed at even that.

Most people don't realize quite what Milan accomplished in beating Crispus Attucks in the semistate, Terre Haute Gerstmeyer in the state semifinals, and Muncie Central in the state finals. Those three teams dominated the fifties, winning five state championships and playing in a total of twelve Final Fours. That Attucks team boasted a sophomore guard named Oscar Robertson, who would become one of the best basketball players in the history of any state. Milan played the best to be the best.

The glory, the memories of that historic moment had begun to fade when *Hoosiers* was released in 1986. To put it mildly, the film wasn't quite what the town and many of the players had in mind. Of all those involved in the actual season, only Ray Craft was in the movie version. He was the representative at Butler Field-house who let the Hickory Huskers into the gym for a practice before the state title game.

Those who lived through the real thing back in 1954 have decidedly different opinions about the fictional version. Almost every person in the town of Milan hated the movie. They complained that it didn't give them any credit, that it strayed too far from the truth, that it made them look like a group of backward hicks. Most of the players loved it, thought it was great that somebody would even want to loosely base a movie on their accomplishments on the basketball court.

The movie–real-life parallels are few but unmistakable. Both teams came from small schools where there was a large emphasis on basketball. Both teams won the championship over a bigger, dominant opponent with a last-second shot. Almost everything else in the movie is fictionalized. For one thing, it makes for better entertainment. For another, no one could ever know exactly what happened.

The townspeople's complaints revolve around the making and the content of the movie. Filmmakers refused to shoot any of the footage in Milan, citing the commercialization. "They didn't have to put the words Milan in there, but I think they should have at least used some picture that came from Milan," said former restaurant owner Rosie Arkenberg.

Many people think the oldtimers were looking for some sort of small-town rebirth from the movie. It never happened. "They were looking for some sort of Milan revival, and they didn't understand that they just wanted to use the basis of the team, not the whole town," said White. "All of us from Milan were looking for a little more Milan. It portrayed the way basketball was in a small town. They'll ask me, 'Who were you?' and I couldn't find myself in there. I would say the movie is probably the reason Milan came back into the forefront. If not for the movie, we would have slowly disappeared like the Franklin Wonder Five."

"I think the oldtimers in Milan were thinking they were going to get in the spotlight again," Engel said. "They thought everybody was going to come into Milan. It was just a nice movie. It wasn't crash, bang and everybody shooting each other. It was a nice movie."

The oldtimers complain that the movie had more of a 1930s setting, that it featured men in bib overalls, that it had dirt roads, that the parallels were very thin. All of those complaints, they say, detracted from Milan's overall image.

"It was just too old," Daren Baker says. "It was really rural and we're rural, but it was much more rural than we were. I think the people on the West Coast must think, 'Wow, what a hick place that must be.' They look at it and think that's probably the way we live in the Midwest, but we don't really care about that."

Most of the Milan players enjoyed the movie. They were just happy that it put their story back in the spotlight.

"I didn't have any feelings that they were infringing on some-thing that was mine," says Craft. "They went through the films, through the state on helicopter. I thought the people who did the movie knew Indiana basketball. It would be very hard to make the exact Milan story. They did a good job of depicting basketball in Indiana."

Says Plump, "I loved it. I thought it was great. The emotions that the movie portrayed caught what the fifties were all about. Everybody knows the movie was about Milan. I don't care whether you're talking about the state of Washington, the Den-ver papers, or the Los Angeles papers. To me, that's pretty signifi-cant. I disagree with the people in Milan on this. I'm very gratified that somebody would even use Milan loosely to make a movie. I think if the people in Milan are disappointed, they're being a little unrealistic in their expectations."

Engel thought the researchers needed to do a little more work. Butte was angry that the Milan players were invited to the world premiere in Indianapolis but were asked to pay $100 for a ticket. "Heck, if it was about you, they would surely invite you to come up and see it without paying a hundred bucks," says Butte. "The first time I saw it I was very disappointed. There was no credit to Milan, there were no scenes from Milan. I was not invited to see any of the filming. After the second time I watched it, I appreci-ated that it was a good movie. I do enjoy watching the movie now."

The movie did bring the team back together. They first gath-ered in the school gymnasium for a pep session and an anniversary tribute. The players then rode in caravan—in Cadillacs, of course—to Batesville, where the town had reserved the entire theater for the first showing of the movie.

That movie told the Milan story, although indirectly, to a new generation. The people who had seen it happen in '54 had not forgotten it, but the movie gave Milan a definite boost in national popularity that no newspaper article could have matched.

Even though he didn't like the movie when it first opened, Butte probably sums up the experience best.

"I think the movie *Hoosiers* did more than any of us will ever realize," he says, "to solidify our niche in history."

Even the movie, though, couldn't do justice to what really happened that year. Any team can win games in movies. This was real life. The oldtimers talk of the day after the tournament finale when 20,000 people crowded into their town to cheer the heroes. They talk of Indianapolis policeman Pat Stark leading the champions home and then crying on a stage before all those people. They talk about how they closed the town the night of the finals so everyone could go to the game. Everyone has his story, and the stories seem to grow bigger every year.

Most of the changes in the lives of those who participated have been good. Basketball gave them opportunities that they never knew existed and opened doors that previously had always been locked. Most never had been to Indianapolis before that 1953 state tournament. For the four who lived in Pierceville, the three-mile trip to Milan on a Saturday night was considered the entertainment for the week.

The players have gone their separate ways, but most attend an annual reunion. It may be the only basketball team ever that holds a reunion every year. They do it, says Gene White, because "of all the teams to ever play basketball, there are none that are closer than we are." One time, the players decided to invite people from the surrounding area to the reunion at the Milan Country Club, the people who had helped make them champions. It was there, legend goes, that longtime supporter Ralph Miller walked in and cried. "To think," he said, "that you guys would want us to come back here for your reunion. That's unheard of."

That Milan victory and the ensuing magic have had a lasting effect on the entire state. What Milan did was convince every small school in every part of the state that winning the whole thing was possible, that any school could conceivably be champion. It won't happen very often, but the important thing is that it can.

Milan and all, there are varied opinions in Indiana about class basketball. Purists say the only way to hold a tourney is to put every school in one draw and let the best team emerge four weeks later. Others say class basketball allows more teams to win championships, creates more balanced competition, and thus keeps the interest at a high level. That works for almost every other state, but not Indiana—certainly not Indiana since Milan. Part of the great lure of Indiana's state tourney is that anybody can beat anybody on a given night. And Indiana's tournament—in income, attendance, and statewide, even national, interest—is the king of them all. There are many reasons why, but the aura of Milan is a strong one.

Unsurprisingly, the men of Milan's miracle are not divided on the subject of enrollment-class basketball for Indiana. "I think class basketball is simply a way for more schools to get trophies," White said. "That's not a reason for doing it. There's nothing wrong with trophies, but if that's all you play for, then you're missing a lot of things."

In Milan, the younger generation hears the stories and hopes that maybe, just maybe, another miracle might take place, that someday before time ends there will be another parade, another celebration, down that main street. Another Milan team will come back from Indianapolis after winning in the monstrous Hoosier Dome, on those same back roads, through all those other small towns that time has forgotten. People will line those highways and wave to the champions. Milan will be a town of conquering heroes again. Marvin Wood will come back, and so will the players. ESPN will interview the new Marvin Wood, the new Bobby Plump, live on "Sportscenter." Business will return. Land values will soar. Times will be good again.

It never hurts to dream, but that is the impossible dream. From zero wins to the state championship? Not likely in the nineties, not when there is such a big gap even between the best teams and the average ones. Time remembers and has reserved a big spot in history for Milan, but it has also moved on.

"When you look back and you look at your ring," Engel says, "there's a figure, there's a date, my name and the year. But that doesn't tell much. It doesn't tell hard work and sacrifice. We weren't out dating girls on Saturday nights. Nobody had a car. You didn't have money. It showed that if you work hard enough and strong enough, a lot of good things can come out of it. When you don't have anything and then all of a sudden you're at the end of the rainbow, you've got something. You had no idea the night when it was all over that this same thing would still be on the top of the pile.''

But that was yesterday, and yesterday truly is gone. Where once there were hundreds, now just a few schools have an enrollment as small as Milan's in 1954.

Many of the people who witnessed the 1954 miracle are now senior citizens. They pass the stories down to another generation, but it's not the same. Being there and hearing about it are two different things. Marc Combs hasn't seen a game in person in over twenty years. Rosie Arkenberg, Barter and Betty Dobson, Daren Baker, Chet Nichols—they rarely attend the games.

They are too old now to reverse Milan's fortunes. About the only thing they can do is reminisce. They can go to the site of the old 1953 gym at the elementary school, or they can make the short drive to Versailles where Milan's 1954 "home" gymnasium is still standing. They can sit in the same seat as in 1954, shut their eyes, and imagine Plump hitting a jumper, White grabbing a rebound, Craft running the offense, Truitt driving the baseline, Engel going up with power inside, Wood shouting commands. All will be good again, like it was many years ago. The reality of the nineties will disappear.

And then they would go home to Milan of today.

It would be easy to poke fun at Milan and Pierceville without ever visiting them, but go there first. Stop in Pierceville and park in the old church lot behind Schroders' store. Look toward the back where they once played those pick-up games. Close your eyes and imagine it. Bobby Plump, Roger Schroder, Glenn Butte, Gene White. Think how small it is and how far they have gone. Think of youth, innocence, and most of all basketball. Can you hear it? That roundball bouncing, both on the ground and off the rim? The sound of the net as they make shot after shot after shot?

Take a drive farther south and stop in one of those cornfields, in a spot where the old water tower is visible. Look at it from afar

27

and think why so many people come from so many places to see it every year. Look around at the farmland and think of a place that still has so much natural beauty. Think of the movie *Field of Dreams*, and then admit that it wouldn't seem impossible for those players to someday walk out of that cornfield and start a game over at the store.

Drive the three miles into Milan and first stand there between those two Baltimore and Ohio Railroad tracks. Stand there on a sunny day and look east first, then turn around and look west. Just stand there. Don't move. Look so hard and so long that your vision becomes blurry, that everything goes to a point. Listen. Nothing but the wind.

Stand there and try to think that everything is not right with the world. It's impossible. Walk away and try to say that this isn't the proverbial best place to raise a family. It's impossible.

Take a walk down to that water tower, the one that says "State Champs 1954." Ignore the weeds on the ground, the rust on the tower, and the "no trespassing" signs. Look up, stare at it, and try to figure out why it means so much after so long. People just can't put it into words. Walk away and try not to have a small chill go down your spine. That's what it's all about.

3 The 1953 Regular Season

First-year Milan basketball coach Marvin Wood knew he was in trouble the first day of practice in October of 1952. The more than fifty boys trying out for the dozen spots on the team were on the floor when Koon Frowkes, truck driver and president of the Milan School Board, approached him on the sidelines.

"We were standing there and the boys were shooting," Wood says. "He said, 'The old coach said this group ought to make it to the Fieldhouse.'" There is only one Fieldhouse in Indiana: Butler. To get there meant winning at least sectional and regional championships. "I thought that was pressure, coming from the president of the school board. They had *never* been to the Fieldhouse before."

The "old coach" was Herman "Snort" Grinstead, and his story is one that people in the Milan area still debate. He was a tall, demanding man in his mid-fifties, popular among the townspeople. He would sit and talk with fans at Arkenberg's or the barbershop or the drugstore. People sometimes considered his methods harsh, but few argued with the results he generated on the court. In the winter of 1951–52, he had a young, talented team, and the future, it seemed, held nothing but promise for Milan.

"Outside of athletics, he was really a nice man," recalls Bob Engel, who played on the varsity as a sophomore that year. "When it came to basketball, he was very tough. A lot of guys were scared to death of him. He knew the game. When somebody wasn't right up on what they were doing, he was on you because he knew you could do better."

It all started that season when county rival Osgood humiliated Milan, 82–40. Grinstead marched into the dressing room, burst into a tirade, pounded his fist against some lockers, and then kicked seven seniors off the team. "It was a horrendous defeat," recalls Bob Plump, who, like Engel, was dressing for varsity games as a sophomore then. "After the game, he was kicking lockers and shouting and I thought, 'What am I even doing in this dressing room?' He just took the seven uniforms away from them."

Grinstead did relent and brought back Rodney Brandes and Ken Bergman, who happened to be the two best seniors on the team. He then moved Plump and Engel into starting roles. What happened next was amazing. Milan, coming off one of its worst defeats in history, edged always powerful Batesville, 41–40. "From that point, we were on our way," says Plump. "We didn't lose very many more games."

Milan wasn't quite as fortunate in the sectional. Plump was home with the flu, Engel played with the flu, and Batesville got its revenge with a nine-point victory. But people looked the other way because two of Milan's best players were sick, and there would be many more victories than losses in this young team's future. Plump and Engel were only sophomores, and the coming classes had some of the best talent in the history of Ripley County.

Some people say Grinstead was the kind of person who always pushed his luck to the limit. It eventually caught up with him.

After the sectional loss, Grinstead did something that school administrators felt they couldn't ignore. He ordered new uniforms without consulting anyone for permission, and the school didn't have enough money to pay the bill. That, along with what some people call personality conflicts with the school superintendent, led to his dismissal as head basketball coach.

"Snort Grinstead was a terrific man," says former school secretary Betty Dobson, who was probably closer to the situation than anyone now living in Milan. "He was a little voluminous, a little dynamic. If he was mad, you knew it. There were definitely two different personalities. There was a little friction between him and the superintendent.

"In the past, the uniform salesman always went directly to the coach. Good or bad, that's the way it was. What happened was that there were some things ordered and, as the bookkeeper, I can tell you there wasn't enough money to pay for them. The coach and the superintendent went to the bank and got a loan to pay the bill. That was the fuel that lit the fire. I can tell you that the bill did get paid, and we had money at the end of the year."

Grinstead lost his job, the townspeople revolted, and the basketball program was in sudden disarray.

"We had protests and we had people come in groups to the school," says Dobson. "They marched up the steps and demanded to talk to the superintendent. The townspeople loved that man. When I look back and reflect, anybody can make an error. You just have to sit down and work it out. I basically think the superintendent handled it wrong. If you aren't given a job description, then you assume what yours is supposed to be. It was too bad they couldn't sit down like educated persons and work it out. I think there were probably a lot of things we really didn't know, but it's water under the bridge now."

Recalls Plump, "I think Mr. Grinstead said he didn't want to go. My feeling when I found out he was going to go was one of sadness. I thought he had done a good job. We were having fun and I was getting to play. I couldn't understand why he wasn't coming back. The community disliked it very much. There were meetings, and they wanted to get rid of the principal and superintendent. They wanted him back. Looking back at my feelings at the time, I would just as soon that he had stayed. I changed my mind during the '53 season."

Marvin Wood even admits that "I probably wouldn't have gone to Milan if I had known the whole story. I was not aware all of this had taken place."

Part of the uncertainty with Wood came because he was just twenty-four years old and relatively unproven as a coach. He had played three years for Tony Hinkle at Butler and had coached two years at French Lick. He had a winning record in those two years at French Lick and was ready for a change.

Wood and his wife, Mary Lou, fell in love with Milan when they came for the interview with the superintendent. "We couldn't believe how clean and neat the community was," he says. "They had just had a clean-up, fix-up, paint-up campaign, and it was really neat."

By the start of practice, Wood knew it would not be easy to win the support of the town and the players. It would be hard enough for a twenty-four-year-old to earn respect at any school, but in Milan the superintendent had just dismissed one of the most popular men in the entire town. It was also a town obsessed with winning, and they knew the team was capable of doing that.

"Any time a coach comes into a community, there's a honeymoon period," Wood says. "People will wait and see how things go. Does the coach fit in? How will he use the talent? Is he going to work in the community? The honeymoon period was not easy at Milan. They still remembered Coach Grinstead and that he had performed well the year before. I told my wife, 'If we don't have success in this community, there are three people who will be out of this town on the front end of a boot—the superintendent, the principal, and the head basketball coach.' "

Says Dobson, "I think Marvin came in with a strike against him. I think he had to prove himself in two ways, not only as a coach and teacher but that he could fit into the community. He had some big shoes to fill."

The first big difference between Wood and Grinstead was in appearance. Grinstead towered over people at 6-2; Wood was about 5-8. Grinstead shouted; Wood spoke softly. Grinstead liked to hang out with the townspeople; Wood was a family and church man, rarely socializing. Each was demanding in his own way—Grinstead by his legendary tirades, Wood by his encouragement, patience, and example. Wood was young enough to practice with the team and show them how to do things; Grinstead was strictly a teacher.

Some people actually thought it was time for a change, that some fresh blood in the program might be good for the young talent.

"I think the big difference between Mr. Grinstead and Mr.

Wood was that Mr. Wood had just come out of college and he was a step up as far as the game of basketball," says Engel. "A lot of people will disagree. Mr. Grinstead went as far as he could go. Mr. Grinstead had the basics, but he couldn't get to the next plateau. With his knowledge, he was limited."

Wood may have had the knowledge, but he didn't make friends very quickly in Milan. In one of his first moves, he closed all Indian practices. That eliminated one of the primary forms of afternoon entertainment for a lot of Milan men. People in the fifties, especially those in Milan, didn't like change. They didn't want some twenty-four-year-old outsider coming into their community and telling them how he would run "their" basketball program. The old coach was established. The new coach was just that—new.

Milan's basketball tradition was a proud one. The Indians had never won a regional game, but they had won the two tourneys that counted—the Ripley County Tournament and the Versailles Sectional. In those days in Milan and a lot of other Indiana communities, a county tourney championship seemed almost as important as a state title, and much more feasible. State titles were for the big schools, the perennial powers. No one expected to play at "The Fieldhouse." The county tourney meant bragging rights over people you saw on a daily basis. It meant rubbing it in for an entire year until the eight schools gathered again the next year at Tyson Auditorium in Versailles.

It's hard to believe that Ripley County once had nine basketball teams—Milan, Versailles, Batesville, Holton, New Marion, Osgood, Sunman, Napoleon, and Cross Plains. Only Milan and Batesville remain from those eight; the others have consolidated to form larger schools. Milan was the first Ripley County team to play in the state tourney. The Indians played in the fourth one in 1914 at Indiana University, losing to eventual champion Wingate in the opening round.

The biggest measuring stick for small-school success in Indiana high school basketball has always been the sectional, and it's no different in Ripley County. Win the sectional and the locals will talk about it forever, even where the schools have long since consolidated. Milan was the only Ripley County team in the 1916 sectional at Seymour, and the Indians lost in the final to the host squad. The tournament site bounced around from Columbus to Rushville to Aurora over the next few years until Ripley County became a permanent venue in 1925. Aurora won that sectional, one that Osgood missed because the principal forgot to turn in the eligibility list to the IHSAA before the deadline.

Milan completed its gym in 1930, hosted the sectional for one year, and lost in the first round to Lawrenceburg. The Indians finally won the sectional in 1932 with a 32–26 defeat of Batesville. The Red Butt–coached Indians won the sectional in 1935 with a 31–21 win over Osgood and repeated a year later with a 23–22 thriller against Batesville. The Indians didn't lead Batesville until a free throw late in the game gave them the final margin of victory. Ironically, that was also the last sectional played in the old Milan gym.

Several different teams earned sectional championships over the next years—Osgood, Sunman, Batesville, Cross Plains, Napoleon. Eventually, every Ripley County team except New Marion captured the prestigious title. Red Butt brought Milan back into the spotlight in 1946 with a 30–29 victory over Sunman. In 1949, Red Anderson began a dominance at Batesville that saw the Bulldogs win four consecutive sectional titles. Batesville defeated Milan in all four of those tournaments—52–40 in 1949, 51–50 in 1950, 50–35 in 1951, and 43–33 in 1952.

A basic parity existed in the early years of Ripley County basketball before bigger and stronger Batesville flexed its muscle in the early fifties. These teams did little, however, beyond the sectional. No team had made it past the regional, let alone the semistate or the state finals in Indianapolis. Marvin Wood inherited a Milan program that had won four sectional titles but had lost its first game all four times in the Rushville Regional. It was also a team its community loved, win or lose. The locals could usually find some reason to blame the referees, the coach, or both.

Kicking the townspeople out of the practices was the first in a series of actions that had them saying, "The old coach didn't do it like that." Wood didn't find that the people were unfriendly. One of their big complaints was that he didn't come to Arkenberg's on Saturday mornings to rehash the games. But Wood had his own agenda, his own way of doing things. He might have been quiet, but it was clear who made the decisions in the basketball program.

"A lot of coaches get themselves in hot water because they go to places where people can be critical and criticize," Wood says. "I never did that. I didn't hang out at the corner drugstore. I didn't hang out at the barbershop. I was more involved in church. I was more involved in school. I was more involved in activities where kids were involved."

One person who took an instant liking to the new coach was Bob Peak, Wood's landlord and self-proclaimed president of the mythical Downtown Coaches Club. They had a regular table at Arkenberg's every Saturday morning. If it was after a Friday-night game, they would critique each player's performance. If it was in the off-season, they would examine the prospects for the upcoming campaign.

The same thing happened in almost every other small town in Indiana. No one knows who started it in Milan, but they were there every Saturday. They had a play for every zone defense invented. Listen to them, and breaking the full-court press was as easy as hitting a layup. Man-to-man defense? No problem, just give it to Plump and let him go one-on-one. They had good intentions, but those intentions often interfered with what the coach—in this case Marvin Wood—was trying to accomplish.

Since he was Wood's landlord, Peak tried to take the new coach under his wing. He tried to tell him how it was in Milan and what those downtown coaches expected.

"When they wanted to get a message to me, it always came through him," Wood said. "He would always say, 'The guys downtown want to know why you don't do this,' or he'd say, 'The guys were wondering why the team didn't do a little better the other night,' or he'd say, 'Are you working up anything new?' It wasn't once or twice a week. He was over at our house every day. At first, it bothered me. It's just like anything else. You get so much of it, you adjust to it."

When Wood was at school during the day, Peak went to the house and gave Mary Lou coaching tips to pass along to her husband that night. "He used to come over every day at noon," Mary Lou recalls, "and I would think that the neighbors were going to talk about him coming over all the time. I said something about it to one of the neighbors, and they said, 'Don't worry about it. When you have him over at your house, that gives all of us a rest.' He was a talker."

The Woods also knew that Peak meant well. "After games he would always talk about how they played," Mary Lou said. "He and his wife always took me to games. He found out I could bake, and he made a deal that if we won, I had to bake him a pie. I got behind when we started winning."

When Wood looked on the court during those tryouts in October of 1952, he knew there was some talent. He probably never imagined, though, that three-fourths of the boys at Milan High School would try out for the team. He was still without an assistant coach, and it would be midway through the season before he brought in Clarence Kelly to coach the junior varsity.

How in the world could he pick a team of so few from a group of so many? Here was a man trying to fit into a community that wanted its old coach back, and he had to tell more than thirty boys that they couldn't play on the basketball team.

"I was really impressed with the talent," Wood says. "Each and every one of them had some talent, had some skill. That was a pleasant sight to a new coach coming into the community. There was quickness, size, and numbers—more size than I had at French Lick, more size than any high school team I had played on. There was almost more size than any college team I had played on."

Always available was longtime junior high coach Marc Combs. A 1933 Milan graduate, Combs spent more than thirty-five years teaching in the Milan school system. He had other opportunities, but his roots always kept him in Milan. "You grew up here," he says. "It's instinct. You'd rather be back with the people you know. I wasn't aiming to teach all of my life. But you get started, and these kids need help. It just draws you to them."

Combs is pictured in most of the championship team photos and claims to be the only junior high coach to have a state championship ring. If any junior high coach should have a ring, it's Combs. He had watched those Milan players since the early years and had helped mold them through the seventh and eighth grades.

Combs is old-school. He has preached fundamentals for more than forty years. He says that separates the great teams from the average ones. "I had the best man in the country for fundamentals in Marc Combs," Engel says.

"You could see that those boys were going to be ballplayers,"

Combs says. "You could see they had a lot of talent. They were in the rough behind the barn playing basketball. You've got to bring them in and make them do the things you want them to do. In that group, you could take one out, put another in, and not lose anything.

"The story I always told them was that they put their shoes on just like you do. You're just as good as you want to be. That always stuck with them. If you've got boys with a brain, with good hands, you can make a ballplayer out of them. There's no reason you can't. We weren't just gifted with special boys at the time. They had to work at it mentally and physically—that the game was theirs if they wanted it."

The players also had a fierce competitive edge, developed by playing against each other. Each summer, the group from Pierceville played the group from Milan in baseball. In the early days, they were friendly enemies instead of teammates. Plump, White, Butte, and Schroder in Pierceville. Craft, Engel, Jordan, Wendelman, Cutter, and Truitt in Milan. Who won? It depends who tells the story.

When those boys finally got together as teammates on the basketball court, they were virtually unstoppable. As sixth-graders, the legend goes, they played the seventh-grade, eighth-grade, ninth-grade, and high school teams during lunch. And won all of those games.

As eighth-graders, they were undefeated heading into the big county tourney. It was in that tourney against Osgood that they received a harsh dose of reality. No one remembers the exact score, but it was bad. Osgood doubled the score on the overconfident Indians, coached by Combs.

"We were crying in the dressing room," Plump recalls, "and I thought the end of the world had come. Marc Combs came in, and I couldn't understand why he wasn't crying. I'll never forget his words. He said, "I know all of you feel bad, but I want you to remember one thing. You have to play. Other teams are never going to lay down because you think you're good. I believe that's what happened to you.' That's all he said. From my standpoint, from that point on, we never took a team lightly. I don't care if we had beaten them fifty points before. It all went back to that eighth-grade thing, and it was probably the best thing that happened to us."

In October 1952, most of the players were juniors and Wood was their coach. A big expectation for Milan basketball in the early fifties was a title in the county tourney and the opportunity to keep the trophy—which had its own name, Vic—for one year. Winning that title for three consecutive years meant keeping Vic for good. No one ever considered a trio of titles. The 1952 squad under Grinstead had won Vic, and people did know that a repeat performance was not impossible. But expect it? About the only thing the town expected was that the Baltimore and Ohio train would come through every afternoon.

What Wood did early in those practice sessions changed the entire look of the Milan team. Not only did he bar outsiders from watching practices, but he also changed the entire offensive and defensive scheme to the Hinkle system that he had learned in his three years at Butler. He stressed man-to-man defense and always ran set plays.

"Coach Grinstead was a run-and-gun type coach," Wood says. "I liked to run, but if we didn't have the break, I liked to play percentage ball. We ran an offensive pattern. This was the first time they had seen an offensive pattern."

After those first few practices, many of the Milan players believed that Wood might just be the answer to some of their problems. They saw that he trusted them, and they returned that trust. It was the beginning of a mutual respect that has carried well into the nineties.

"Wood could personally demonstrate what he wanted done," says Craft. "He stressed the Butler system. It is a system which breaks down to teach the basic fundamentals of basketball. They [Wood and Grinstead] had different personalities, and the way they taught the game, the way they approached the game was different."

"When basketball started, he [Wood] made a difference," says Gene White. "Instead of telling you how to do something, he showed you how to do it. Mr. Grinstead said that on defense, you play between your man and the basket. Mr. Wood said that, too, but he showed you how to do it. It wasn't overwhelming to start with because Mr. Grinstead was well liked."

While Grinstead coached at nearby Moore's Hill, Wood prepared to begin his first season at Milan. The 1952–53 Milan squad is often the forgotten team, one embraced by the town as it made its own miraculous run to the Final Four, but also one shoved forever into the background when the Indians won the state in '54.

The story of the '53 team might be more important and more unbelievable than that of the squad that actually won the state a year later. There were no expectations, beyond a possible county tourney championship. "There were some expectations that we could win the sectional, but I don't know about much more than that," Craft says. "I think people would have been satisfied had we won the sectional and just played well at the regional."

Wood relied on a core of players in most games, with the starting five usually featuring four juniors and one senior. Jim Wendelman, a strong 6-4, 210-pound senior center, anchored Milan's powerful inside game. Says Wood, "Not only was he well put together but he was pretty agile. He could run and he could jump. A guy like that is going to make a contribution to your team." Wendelman was flanked by Ronnie Truitt and Gene White. Engel and Plump combined to form the guard tandem. Craft was often one of the first players off the bench, and Ralph Preble was the only senior besides Wendelman who saw much action that season. It was basically a junior team, a team of the future, but it had its sights set squarely on the present.

Milan opened the season before a capacity home crowd against county rival Sunman and won easily, 62–38, led by seventeen points from Plump. Wood was relieved that the anxiety of opening night had ended with a win, but he realized there was a very long road ahead. The Indians also rolled the next night, a twenty-one-point victory over Rising Sun. The real story in this game, however, was that Rising Sun led 15–11 after the first period and trailed just 26–23 at halftime. That's when Wood made a move that would prove valuable both in that game and down the road. He switched from the traditional man-to-man to a zone, which Milan had never practiced. Rising Sun never recovered.

"The boys knew I had made a major adjustment," Wood recalls. "They had made adjustments in learning the offense. We both made adjustments early in the season. They accepted me because I wasn't a know-it-all. I accepted them because they made adjustments to my style. The chemistry became good between me and the team. Of course, when you win, the chemistry is always good between the coach and the team."

Wood's honeymoon ceased briefly. At Vevay, Milan lost for the first time under him, 56–54. Milan overcame a seven-point deficit in the first half to take a 45–44 lead into the fourth quarter, but Vevay battled back to win. Four nights later came the most telling sign of future success. Milan won 55–43 at Batesville, the nemesis that had knocked Milan out of the previous four sectionals. A mental barrier tumbled; Milan *could* play with the bigger, stronger teams in the area. And win.

The Indians followed with five consecutive wins over Osgood, North Madison, Brookville, Holton, and Hanover. The closest game was 41–35 over Holton. Then the road got tougher, the teams bigger and stronger. Aurora outscored Milan 19–7 in the final quarter to break the winning streak and win 51–40. Milan had led until midway through the fourth period in a game billed by the Versailles *Republican* as indicating "the regional possibilities of Milan, still the best team in Ripley County." Lawrenceburg followed that with a 54–44 win that dropped the Indians to 8–3 and reduced tournament expectations. Everyone knew that Aurora and Lawrenceburg could provide big roadblocks later in potential regional matchups.

Wood's Milan honeymoon definitely was over. He began to hear questions and criticisms. He discovered that the amiable small town he had encountered a few months earlier liked to win basketball games more than it liked to make new friends.

"We lost those games early and they really got on him," Plump recalls. "When we started winning, they thought he was the greatest coach in the world. I talk to those people now and I say, 'Do you remember when you didn't like Woody?' and they say, 'It wasn't me.' I can't find any of those people now. They're not around."

They aren't around because Wood did indeed begin to win consistently. The Indians went into the holidays with a 64–54 win over Versailles that ended the two-game skid. New Year's Eve was one holiday that Plump and Jim Wendelman would probably like to forget. Because of the holiday, Wood extended the normal curfew until 1:00 A.M. He also told each player that he would check on him shortly after that curfew time and that any violations would result in a three-game suspension.

What happened next depends on who tells the story. Wood did catch Wendelman as he took someone home after 1:00 A.M.

Whether or not he caught Plump breaking the training rules depends on an interpretation of the facts. Plump double-dated with classmate Bill Rainer that night, and the two ended up at Versailles State Park well past midnight. Here's where the situation gets a little confusing.

"It's probably the only mistake Marvin Wood made as a coach, and it was a mistake," Plump contends. "This is the honest-to-God truth. I never had a problem with training. I was never out late. I didn't drink. I didn't smoke. I was normally right on time. He said he was going to check on everyone, and that there was nothing you could do after one that you couldn't do before one. We ended up at Versailles State Park. We left the park in time to get home by taking the shortcut, and we honest to God had a flat tire. I said, 'I've *got* to get home.' We changed it and pulled up in front of our house at either five or ten to one. I remember thinking, 'I'm here. Everything is fine.'

"Now, there's not much traffic in Pierceville at one in the morning. I saw this car come up and turn down our road. I had a vague idea that maybe it was Marvin, but we were sitting in front of my house. He drove by, turned around, and parked parallel to my car. When he drove by, the thought crossed my mind, 'Plump, you better get in the house.' But I thought I was okay there. He said, 'What time have you got?' I said, 'One o'clock.' He said, 'I've got five after.' I said, 'Woody, we had a flat tire, honest to God. You can still feel it.' He said, 'You should have planned ahead for it. See me before the next game.' "

Wood contends it was just after one when he saw his star guard outside the house. He also says that he drove by the house to the end of the street because he was "trying to figure out what to do."

The coach did nothing at first, conducting the usual practices in preparation for Milan's next game with county rival Napoleon. When they went home on Thursday night, Plump and Wendelman expected to play in the game. Things worked out a little differently.

"He didn't say anything in practice, so I packed my bag for the game," Plump says. "I came in early and went into the dressing room and was sitting on the table. He was on the other side of the room. His first words were, 'Bob I think I need to make an example out of you. You can't play tonight. You can't even sit on the bench tonight.' I remember Jim Wendelman coming up and saying, 'He got me at three in the morning.' Everybody would come by in the stands and say, 'What are you doing up here?' "

By the end of the night, Wood looked like a genius. He had made his point in benching two stars, and the Indians still won, 64–52. White led the way with nineteen points. Craft scored fourteen, Truitt thirteen, Bill Jordan and Engel eight each, and Schroder two. "You realized your star and your best scorer was out and your best rebounder was out too," White says. "With all of those things, you kind of go above and beyond what you normally do." Says Plump, "You always wanted your team to win, but here were your starting guard and your starting center in the stands. And I'll be damned if they didn't beat Napoleon by twelve points."

Wood also delivered the message to the rest of the team. It served as a reminder about who made the rules, and also who enforced them. "That was an eye-opener for everyone," Schroder says. "I don't know that I was surprised. He just backed up what he said." He did relent somewhat the next week when he agreed to lift the remaining two games of the suspension if Plump and Wendelman each ran a hundred laps around the Milan gymnasium. They ran the laps and were in uniform for that weekend's county tournament. "The reason I think he didn't kick us off for three games was that the county tournament was coming up," Plump laughs.

Milan had little trouble winning its second consecutive county title. The Indians routed Sunman, 59–30, and then dismantled Napoleon, 51–33, in the semifinals. Four players—White, Truitt, Wendelman, and Plump—hit double figures in the first game, while Plump led with fourteen points against Napoleon. The Indians jumped to a 20–6 lead in the finals against Versailles and never looked back in a 68–45 victory. White scored fifteen points to pace the winners.

The Indians won four of their remaining five games, the lone defeat 60–57 to North Vernon. The closest of the four victories was an eleven-point margin over Versailles in a rematch of the county tournament finals.

That sent Milan into the state tournament with a 17–4 record, the best in Ripley County but still not good enough to ensure a victory in the sectional. In a tradition in Ripley County, the cheerleaders of each school penned a tribute to their team before the sectional that appeared in the Versailles *Republican*. The Milan report for 1953, prepared by Joan Johnson, Virginia Voss, and Eleanor Voss, read:

The following is a resume of the activities concerning the Milan Indians:

Jim (Big Jim) Wendelman is a senior. He has played two years of fine ball. He plays center and is noted for his proficient rebounding.

Bob (Curley) Engel is a junior. This is his second year on the varsity. One of his specialties is long set shots.

Ronnie (Stretch) Truitt is a junior. He is one of the best rebounders in the county. His set shots from the corner are excellent.

Bobby (Ker) Plump is a junior. This is also his second year on the varsity. He is noted for his fine driving ability and his excellent jump shots.

Gene (Whitey) White is a junior. His specialties are rebounding and tip ins. He also excels in his jump shots.

Raymond (Flash) Craft is a junior. He is one of the fastest guards around. His driving ability is very good.

Ralph (Prebs) Preble is a senior. He has played three years of fine ball. His jump shots are the hardest to stop.

Kenny (Dimples) Wendelman is a junior. He is one of the finest and toughest rebounders and will always give a good performance to the end.

Jim (Harry) Call is a senior. He plays a very hard ball game, is a hard rebounder and is a dead shot.

Roger (Rog) Schroder is a junior. He is noted for his excellent drive in lay up ability and for his set and jump shots.

Dale (Smitty) Smith is a junior. He is one of the hardest playing guards in the county and plays the game for all it's worth.

Bill (Al) Jordan is a sophomore. His specialty is rebounding and his driving from the corner is outstanding.

Coach Marvin Wood has displayed excellent ability in guiding and securing the utmost performance of his talented and successful team. His untiring efforts merit the high esteem of his boys and loyal fans.

At mid-season, **Clarence Kelly Jr.** assumed the duties of the mentor of the reserve team and deserves honorable mention because of the record of his enviable team.

For a number of years **Marc Combs** has been grade team coach and has done a magnificent job in that capacity. Last but not least our student managers, **Fred Busching** and **Ralph Williamson**, deserve credit for their hard work, cooperation and dependability. Braves, warriors, chiefs, squaws and papooses will be striving for the championship goal.

This was the team that most people thought would win the sectional. Few really believed Milan could go any farther in the state tournament. The Indians drew Osgood in the first round of the Versailles Sectional on Friday night. That meant the Indians would need to win three games in twenty-four hours to win the tournament.

• • •

The expectations were a little different in Muncie in March of 1953. Muncie Central was trying to do what only one team in the tournament's storied history had done: win three straight state championships. The Franklin team that had done it in 1920, '21, and '22 was and still is known reverently as the "Wonder Five." The Bearcats had already won twenty sectionals, ten regionals, and four state titles. They had an all-time record of 703 victories against just 294 setbacks. Success wasn't something that came around every once in a while. It was there on a permanent basis.

Art Beckner guided Muncie Central to the 1951 state championship, but left following the season to take a pay increase as coach of North Central Conference rival and neighbor Richmond, which had a young football-basketball star named Lamar Lundy and expected big things. The Bearcats lured Jay McCreary, who had played on Frankfort's 1936 state high school champions and Indiana's 1940 NCAA champions, from his position as head coach at DePauw University to take over the program for the 1951–52 season. On paper, it seemed like a difficult task. The Bearcats, who had lost their top players—six in all—played one of the tougher schedules in the state. But McCreary didn't have to think long about the offer.

"It was one of the best jobs in the state," McCreary said. "The fans were really crazy about it. They were fantastic. They were behind you 100 percent. It was very important to the school. Athletics in high school were a big part of everybody's life. I don't think they overemphasized it. If you had a good sports team, it was a pride factor. In Muncie, you never planned a basketball banquet until after the state finals. They expected you to do well all of the time. Some schools do well and then disappear. Muncie Central was consistent year in and year out."

In his first Muncie season, 1951–52, McCreary brought with him a running, fast-paced game, a big contrast to the departed Beckner. Muncie Central won its first four games under McCreary before losing a bitter game to Richmond and Beckner. A six-game winning streak followed, before a second loss to South Bend Central. Then, the Bearcats lost three of their last eight games to finish the regular season at 15–5, an excellent record at most schools but just average for Muncie Central.

The tourney was a different case. Tradition, recent and ancient, made Muncie Central tournament-tough. The team had fully adapted to McCreary's system by March. The Bearcats raced through the sectional, the closest contest a fifteen-point decision over Muncie Burris in the finals. They then avenged that earlier loss to Richmond with a 50–39 win in the final game of the regional. Things weren't as easy in the next two rounds. Muncie Central slipped past Auburn and Kokomo in the semistate and then edged New Albany 68–64 in the afternoon game of the state finals. That set up a North Central Conference final between Muncie Central and Indianapolis Tech, a team the Bearcats had defeated, 69–46, earlier in the season. The final was almost a replay of that regular-season game. Muncie Central won, 68–49, to capture its second straight championship.

"There were a lot of sophomores and juniors on the team," McCreary said. "They had some talent and they liked to run. It was a case of having talent and just hoping. I was at the right place at the right time."

So McCreary and Muncie Central went into 1952–53 optimistic and confident. The Bearcats had lost just two double-digit scorers from the '52 team and looked like a solid favorite to turn the hat trick.

Muncie Central was invincible during the first two months of the season. It won twelve straight games, including two narrow victories over rival Richmond, considered by many the best team in the state. Reality set in with two consecutive losses, 70–67 to South Bend Central and 38–27 to Indianapolis Tech, but the Bearcats stormed back to win the last six games and enter the tournament 18–2—in great position to start their quest for history. Given the way they had dominated the regular season and their two consecutive titles, the Bearcats became the team to beat that March.

"We had the best ballclub in the state that year," McCreary said.

He still had to prove it in the tournament.

4 *The 1953 Tournament*

The biggest question facing the Milan Indians heading into the 1953 Versailles Sectional was whether the 55–43 regular-season victory meant they could shed the Batesville tournament stigma—four straight sectional losses.

"We thought we were the best team in the county, and we thought we could win the sectional," said Gene White. The only problem was that many other Milan teams had entered the sectional with the same thoughts, often ended by larger and more powerful Batesville.

"We didn't think in terms of how far you can go," said Bob Engel. "As far as going to the state finals, I don't think we ever thought about that. There was tough competition in the county. They made you work hard."

Said Roger Schroder, "Indianapolis and the state championship were removed from our day-to-day living. We knew we were pretty good because we were beating everybody in the eighth grade. Everybody had talked about what a good team we could be. But I don't think anybody in the Ripley County area set sights very high because Milan had never won a game in the regional.''

Before they could try to win that first game in the regional, the Indians had three games to play at Versailles in the sectional. It turned out that Milan had little to worry about, winning 51–23 over Osgood, 26–15 over Holton, and 42–27 against Batesville in the championship. Next came perhaps the biggest mental hurdle Milan would face—playing in the regional. Knowing the school had never won a regional game made the preparation and pressure even more difficult.

The Indians drew Morton Memorial, a tiny school for orphans in northern Rush County, named for the state's Civil War governor. The game turned out to be one of the most controversial in regional history. A newspaper account called it ''the biggest rhubarb in the 28 years of regional tourneys here.''

Milan led 14–9 after the first quarter. Then the underdog Tigers, popular with the crowd, went ahead 27–26 at the half, 35–34 after three quarters, a stunningly sudden, apparently insurmountable 45–36 with just over two minutes left.

Then, fate: the scoreboard clock malfunctioned. It wasn't noticed right away, so time literally stood still as Milan came charging back. Ray Craft tied the game at 49–49 to force overtime, and the Indians won, 53–51, in two overtimes.

The first regional tournament victory ever for Milan was bittersweet. Tainted. The talk between afternoon and evening sessions was of the points that Milan had scored while the clock didn't move—probably more than twenty crucial seconds, most reporters estimated.

''It did occur. That's a fact,'' Plump says. ''I spoke at a luncheon about three years ago. After I spoke, a man came up to me and said he was the timer that day and the clock would not start.''

Schroder said, ''When I was coaching at Indianapolis Marshall, a kid came up to me. He said, 'You were on the team that won the state championship?' I said I was in the right place at the right time. He said, 'So you're the one that stole that regional from us orphans down there at Morton Memorial.'

''I knew that it wasn't looking good, and I was amazed at how many points we caught up in a short period of time. It was just unbelievable. We used a full-court zone press, double-teaming the ball and taking out the passing alleys. People just didn't do that back then. The zone press stuff was unheard of. They just lost their composure."

It remains the only sectional championship in Morton Memorial history.

Milan had only a few hours to shake off the exhilaration and pathos of the Morton Memorial game before an evening showdown with Connersville for the regional championship. Afternoon results seemed to give Milan no chance. While Milan had struggled with Morton Memorial, Connersville had whipped Aurora. "Their team was just beautiful," Wood said of Connersville.

Most people thought nothing could top that afternoon fiasco with Morton Memorial. They were wrong.

The game with Connersville marked the first real impact of Milan's "cat-and-mouse" game. Milan led 8–4 after the first quarter, and Connersville missed a shot to open the second period. Plump brought the ball upcourt, stopped, and held it—for almost eight minutes. The crowd, the majority Connersville fans, reacted angrily. In Indiana, basketball generally meant run and gun. "Cat-and-mouse" meant stall, which to fastbreak connoisseurs meant chickening out. These fans had watched Connersville run to high scores all season, and now their team was helpless. The only action in the second quarter was by Connersville fans, who threw coins and debris onto the court.

"Truitt was walking around picking up money, and Plump was standing there holding the ball," Engel laughs. "You tell people stuff like that today and they don't believe you. If Truitt were alive, he could probably tell you how much money he picked up."

Engel had no sympathy for the outraged fans or their team. "We played ball control that game. We brought the ball to halfcourt. If they wanted it, they could come and get it. They didn't have the pressure defense to do that."

White said, "Plump just held the ball, and the rest of us would go over to the corner and do exercises to keep warm."

In a preview of his Game of Fame, Plump held the ball for the final shot of the half—and missed it. He converted the miss into a rebound basket that gave the Indians a 10–4 lead at the half.

The game opened up in the third quarter, but Milan still led 17–15 going into a wild fourth quarter. The score was tied twice and the lead changed six times. Craft's long jumper tied the game

49

at 22, and his layup with just over five seconds remaining gave Milan a 24–22 victory. "We shouldn't have beaten Connersville," White said. "That was a tremendous upset. Things just kind of fell into place for us."

Wood remembers, "There were some experiences we went through in that game that you don't go through in a regular basketball game. The crowd was very vocal because we were holding the ball. The real nasty part came at the end of the game. They walked by our bench and spit on us, and called us everything you could think of.

"There was not good blood for a long time between Connersville and Milan. When I was coaching at New Castle, we went to play at Connersville. Their crowd started chanting, 'Hold that ball. Hold that ball.' We were just warming up. They got ahead of us in that game and *they* held the ball. Milan played them again in the regional a couple of years later and there was still not good blood."

But there was joy in Milan, celebrating the first regional championship in its history. In between smiles, the subject was the stall. How did Wood come up with the idea? How could such a young coach so effectively use such a potent weapon? Most of all they wondered: How did it work?

"The Milan stall and cat-and-mouse possession game is speedily becoming a feared maneuver in Ripley County," wrote Leroy Hartman under the pen name of Bunny Shot in the Cincinnati *Enquirer*. "It appears more aggravating to the fans than to the players. Bunny doesn't like the stall but we think the passing game in which the players maneuver for openings to drive in for layups is a move back to real basketball. To us, it is an evidence of good coaching. We never were an advocate of the run-and-shoot tactics."

Milan now found itself in unfamiliar territory. The Indians were going to Indianapolis to play Attica in the second game of the semistate. Most of the Milan players had never been to Indianapolis. Most didn't know the location of Attica—the entire width of the state away from Milan. What they did realize was that they had a favorable draw, because powerhouses Indianapolis Crispus Attucks and Shelbyville faced each other in the opening game.

The Indian players might have been a little bit in awe, but they were not afraid. "As you beat teams and win, you start to understand the stature of those teams," said Craft. "We beat some pretty good-sized schools. I don't think we were afraid of playing anybody. I think every game we went into, we thought we had a shot at winning."

The unexpected happened in the first game when Shelbyville upset semistate favorite Attucks, 46–44, in what Wood termed "one of the most marvelous coaching jobs I've seen in my life" by Shelbyville's Frank Barnes. Six years earlier Barnes had coached Shelbyville to its only state championship with a final-game upset of unbeaten Terre Haute Garfield and future Kansas All-American Clyde Lovellette.

Milan and Attica didn't let the Butler Fieldhouse fans down in the second game.

One thing about Milan's march to the state finals in 1953 was that none of the games was boring. The Indians and Attica were tied at 29 at halftime, at 45 at the end of regulation. White hit two free throws with nine seconds left in overtime to give Milan a 49–46 lead and seal the victory. A last-second field goal by Attica made no difference.

Either Milan or Attica would have expected to play Attucks for the semistate title on Saturday night, and either would have been expected to lose big. It was a totally different story with Shelbyville. There are two theories about what happened in that championship game. Either Milan was so well prepared that it would have dominated Shelbyville any night, or Shelbyville just didn't have anything left after beating Attucks in the afternoon.

The final score was Milan 43, Shelbyville 21.

Milan center Jim Wendelman dominated the game. He controlled the boards, and he was a major reason why Shelbyville hit just two field goals in the entire game. Those two field goals remain the lowest semistate total since 1936, the first year there were semistates.

"Wendelman set the tone for that game," said Wood. "Shelbyville had a very talented center. One of the first plays of the game, he made a move to the basket, and Big Jim smashed his shot against the backboard and pulled it down. That guy never tried anything again. That one play seemed to give Big Jim control inside."

According to Engel, "Wendelman played the best game you

could play that day. We held one of the best teams at the time to just two field goals in the entire game. That's hard to believe. Jim Wendelman controlled the boards at both ends of the court.

"That was the best game he ever played in his life. He was an old farm boy. . . . He never played basketball until he was a freshman in high school. He went out for baseball and asked the coach, 'Do you have any left-handed bats?' I still get on him about that."

Bunny Shot wrote the next day, "The Indians of Milan went to town! And it will be a long time before Indianapolis forgets it. . . . What the Indians did to Shelbyville just shouldn't happen to a regional winner. They passed the Bears dizzy, opening up holes that from the press row looked big enough for a truck to go through for layups. Led by Jim Wendelman, they swept both backboards. Generaled by Bob Plump, they had the Bears driving and stumbling in efforts to break up the passing game—and the fans at the fieldhouse loved it—all except Shelbyville."

The victory over Shelbyville touched off a wild celebration in Milan. The parade of cars from Indianapolis stopped for a couple of victory laps around the town square in Shelbyville. It arrived back in Milan about 1:00 A.M. for a bonfire, a pep session, and a rehashing of the game for those who had stayed home.

"They were on cloud nine," Wood said of the townspeople. "They were living a dream. I knew we were in the Final Four, but I knew we really weren't a Final Four–type team. It was a real dream. They had never won a regional game, and there they were in the Final Four."

• • •

Muncie Central coach Jay McCreary had already proclaimed his team the best in the state in 1953. Few could argue with him heading into the tournament. After all, the Bearcats had won the past two state titles.

No team came close to Muncie Central in the sectional. The Bearcats breezed 94–30 over Albany, 58–36 over Center, 65–31 over Yorktown, and 66–47 over Muncie Burris. They opened the regional by routing Parker, 78–50. The Bearcats were playing so well it seemed like the state tournament might be only another formality.

There was, however, a neighborhood battle to settle. Conference rival Richmond was No. 3 in the polls, Muncie Central No. 1. Richmond had Art Beckner, who had coached Muncie Central's 1951 state champs. And Richmond had Lamar Lundy, who was fearsome in a basketball uniform.

The Bearcats had defeated Richmond once in conference play (52–51) and again in a holiday tourney (62–59). An Indiana high school basketball adage said that one good team wouldn't beat another good team three times. McCreary had heard that and scoffed at it. "You beat a team twice and you should beat them again," he said. "I didn't worry about things like that."

He should have worried. It took two overtimes, but in sudden death, Richmond upset the reigning champions, 54–52. It was the first tournament loss in the three-year careers of Charlie Hodson, Jerry Lounsbury, and Tom Raisor. It was also the first tourney defeat for McCreary at Muncie Central.

"It was frustrating," McCreary said. "Things just didn't materialize. I guess everything comes out in the end. Beat me today and I'll beat you tomorrow."

Tomorrow was next season.

• • •

Before 1953, few people in Indiana even knew the location of Milan. Some maps didn't label it. Suddenly, state finals week, the town found itself the focus of the entire state. Forget about South Bend Central, Milan's opponent in the first game, or Richmond or Terre Haute Gerstmeyer. Those were big schools. Everyone wanted to know about the little guy.

Sportswriters from most major daily papers in the state converged on Milan in the week preceding the finals. It was a new experience for both Wood and the players. No one had ever wanted much more than the scores of their games. Now the media wanted their life histories. Writers interviewed the barbers, the shop owners, the farmers, the parents. Everyone with a remote connection to the town suddenly received celebrity status. One headline read, "Ripley Farmers, Townspeople Rally behind Milan."

Superintendent Willard Green even became a basketball expert. "The boys played an inspired game against Shelbyville," he told a reporter. "In fact, they've played a completely different brand of ball ever since the sectionals. The bigger the other teams come, the smaller we seem to make them look."

The Versailles *Republican* received a letter from Daily E. McCoy, Milan's first coach. McCoy wrote:

"Tell the Milan folks the Milan Basketball Team has a lot of boosters up this way, too. I had the privilege of starting the game of basketball in the Milan schools in the year 1914. That year Tommy Thompson, Toner Overly, Arthur Allen, Wallace Rupp and Chris Volz played in the state tournament at Bloomington. We played the famous winning team of Wingate. Wingate held the State Championship for 2 years. It's Milan for me and my house.

"Fraternally yours, Daily E. McCoy."

Things were so bad at one point that Milan resident Will Haney wrote a letter to the Indianapolis *Star* giving a travelogue description of Milan:

> Milan is 39 miles west of Cincinnati on the main line of the B&O St. Louis–to–New York, with commuting trains daily from Milan to Cincinnati. The National and Diplomat crack trains stop on signal. Milan has a population of 1,114, its sister town is Mooreshill (two miles east and population 606), the former home of the old Mooreshill College.
>
> Milan has a furniture and veneer factory; the Whitlach hospital with a fine staff of doctors and nurses; the prettiest nine-hole golf course in the state; a fine lake with cottages; Seagrams' million-barrel warehouse; a first-run movie theater; baseball park with a team in the Tri-County League; four churches (Methodist, Baptist, Catholic, Holiness); new Legion home; St. Charles Amusement Building.
>
> Milan is on Highway 1 and 350, has a fine school and a heck of a good basketball team and coach. It is a rich farming community. Most of the people work at the distilleries, Fisher Body in Hamilton, O., and the Jefferson Proving Grounds in Madison. The Milan Bank is so full that they will rebuild this spring. There is no poverty in Milan; everybody has plenty of money, new cars and fine homes.

The final sentence may have stretched the truth, but the description of Milan was generally accurate as the Indians prepared for the '53 state finals. The papers featured Mary Lou Wood and the cheerleaders. Insurance salesman Red Smith printed 6,000 bumper stickers reading "Go Big Indians." The town planned a welcoming parade for the day following the state, and also passed a resolution concerning the finals:

> WHEREAS, by winning the Semi-Final Championship, the basketball team and the coach has made an additional outstanding achievement and has brought great honor in sports fame to the Milan Public School in the Town of Milan and surrounding communities which the Milan Public School serves. NOW THEREFORE BE IT RESOLVED BY THE BOARD OF TRUSTEES OF THE TOWN OF MILAN, that Saturday, March 21, 1953, be, and the same is, hereby proclaimed a legal holiday for the Town of Milan and respectfully ask the cooperation of all business places and citizens of said Town and the surrounding communities which the Milan Public School District serves to comply with this resolution in honor and appreciation to the team, coaches and officials of the Milan Public School and that all citizens give their active support to the team and coaches in their final elimination contest to be conducted on that date.

Principal Richard Brollier put Milan's allotment of 950 tickets on open sale at the school and the drugstore. That was a mistake. They were gone before Brollier realized he hadn't held any back for priority people, such as players' parents. In Muncie, they knew how to handle the sale of state tournament tickets. In Milan, they didn't. Not only parents but also other deserving people had to hustle for tickets, and Principal Brollier was the man blamed. He had assumed 950 tickets would be more than enough for everyone interested in attending the game. He was wrong, and he paid for it. "He really got into hot water over it," Wood said. "He didn't know any different. He hadn't been in the situation before."

Down in the Milan gymnasium, Wood was an affable interview subject, at least for the early part of the week. He told reporters that most of the tournament revenue would benefit sports other than basketball. "Maybe someday we might even have bowling and tennis," he quipped.

Indianapolis *News* sportswriter J. E. O'Brien wrote: "Other stories have dwelled on Milan's give-and-go offense. . . . This yarn should go more into the boys' lives and their interests outside basketball." O'Brien said that Jim Wendelman spent most of his free time at the Indianapolis semistate "prowling around used-car lots." He said White wanted to be a big-league catcher, and that Ron Truitt liked roller skating and dancing. Bill Jordan, he wrote, "plays saxophone and piano with the Four Aces, a swing combo that furnishes music for the American Legion dance each week and for the annual Fireman's Ball." (Jordan made the comment at the time, "In basketball season, it doesn't make any difference that I can't play on Saturday night—everyone goes to the ballgames instead of the dance anyhow.")

The real story was basketball, and even Wood couldn't avoid it for long. A formidable lineup assembled at Indianapolis: 24–4 Milan, 22–5 South Bend Central, 24–4 Richmond, and 30–3 Terre Haute Gerstmeyer. Richmond, with future pro football Hall of Famer Lundy dominant around the backboards, had powered through the semistate. South Bend Central, with a guard named Jack Quiggle who became all–Big Ten at Michigan State, had downed Logansport and Gary Wallace in the semistate to earn its berth in the finals. Gerstmeyer, led by twins Arley and Harley Andrews and their younger uncle Harold Andrews—all in the Indiana Basketball Hall of Fame now—overcame a sixteen-point halftime deficit to edge Evansville Harrison 78–71 in the semistate.

Milan left a rousing pep session on Friday morning for Indianapolis, where the team stayed at the Pennsylvania Hotel near the downtown area. It was far removed from the excitement of Butler Fieldhouse. "I didn't want them staying in a hotel where there was going to be a lot of traffic, so we just found this little hotel," Wood said. The players also began a tradition that would carry into the 1954 state finals when they ate every meal at the nearby Apex Grill.

"Till I die, I'll never forget going to that restaurant," White says. "They served steak. We were poor; we ate pork or chicken all the time. They came out with a regular meat platter covered with steaks. I had never seen a steak that size in my life. I thought that playing basketball really paid off."

The morning of the finals, as Wood well remembers, didn't go exactly the way the coach of a state finalist team would wish for. "That was the worst morning I can remember," Wood says. "Our kids were beginning to feel their oats a little bit. They were having squirt-gun fights. One of the managers broke off one his teeth; one of the players got his hand caught in the trunk lid.

"We were late getting to Butler Fieldhouse. When we went out to warm up, Plump runs out and bumps somebody and his nose starts bleeding. We weren't in a very good mental frame of mind when that game started. Everything went wrong in our game-day preparations."

Most everything also went wrong in the game against South Bend Central. Bob Collins wrote in the Indianapolis *Star,* "The road ended for Cinderella at Butler Fieldhouse yesterday afternoon." In the first quarter, Milan hit just two of ten field goals, while South Bend connected on six of sixteen. At the half, Milan had hit just five of its twenty-one shots. It didn't get much better in the second half, and the result was a blowout: South Bend Central 56, Milan 37.

"To me, it wasn't that we didn't win the state championship," says Schroder. "We didn't really look that far down the line. It's like when you're playing golf and you have five pars in a row, so you tell your buddy, 'I've got five pars in a row.' What are you going to do on the next one? You're going to blow it because you're not concentrating. I think it was a simple approach for us because we lived simple lives. It wasn't what if we don't win the state. It was just whoever we played next we were going to try to beat. I don't remember anyone talking about winning the state. It didn't take anyone long to realize that it was spectacular to get that far. Had we not won the next year, they'd still be talking about it in Milan. It wouldn't have made the same impact around the state and the nation, but it would have been the best team out of Ripley County ever."

Plump remembers being "terribly disappointed we got beat as badly as we did. I liked the excitement and I wanted to go back, but it wasn't a burning daily thought process."

The loss didn't dampen the celebration. The Milan coaches and players returned home on Sunday to one of the biggest parades in the town's history. A huge caravan of vehicles made the thirteen-mile journey from Penntown to Milan, and a crowd estimated at about 2,000 lined the roadsides. The town later hosted a celebration dinner and banquet with Indiana University basketball coach Branch McCracken, whose team had just won the NCAA championship, as the guest speaker.

The Versailles *Republican* ran this editorial following the tourney:

The Milan high school basketball team certainly put the town of Milan and Ripley County on the map in Indiana the last four weeks. Many Hoosier basketball fans squinted on the map of Indiana to try to locate where Milan was situated.

Milan was the smallest school to reach the finals since 1915, when Montmorenci was there. The enrollment of Milan high school is only 156, while Central of South Bend, their opponent in the finals Saturday afternoon, has 1800 students and 1000 of those students are boys. Milan high school has only 75 boys.

The boys who played on the Milan Indians squad this year played the game to the best of their ability at all times and they never gave up at any time during the tournament.

Their heroic deeds in the Rushville regional tourney will be remembered by every person who had the privilege to witness the ball games, when they brought the first game out of the fire and won the ball game in a double overtime.

Their brilliant efforts against Connersville in the final game of the regional tourney will be remembered by all of the small schools in Indiana for years to come.

The Indians were not given a chance in the Indianapolis Semi-finals by the experts, however they defeated Attica in an overtime in the afternoon and gave the Shelbyville Golden Bears one of the worst defeats they have ever received in tournament play.

It would be very difficult to single out any one player as a hero in the tourney. We believe the best way to describe the victors is as a wonderful team as a whole.

The coaching of Marvin Wood was superb to say the least. He was the calmest man in the gym at all times and never let his boys become rattled on the floor. He always had his boys in hand and the way he encouraged his team, when they were behind in the contests, was magnificent.

We want to congratulate the assistant coaches, Clarence Kelly and Marc Combs, for their untiring efforts and also the student managers and the cheer leaders for a job well done,

We know that all the citizens of Ripley County want to congratulate the Milan basketball team for putting Milan and Ripley County on the front pages of every newspaper in Indiana and bringing glory to their school and town that could not be bought at any price.

Many of the largest daily newspapers in the United States carried stories on their front pages about the Cinderella team from Milan and the people's choice to win the State Tourney crown.

Yes, it was a job well done. The citizens of the Milan community can be proud for years to come of their basketball team of 1953.

Some giddy Milan residents were not disappointed that the team had failed to win the state title because they knew that most of the players would return the next fall. Then the process would simply start anew. A year of experience, they thought, would simply make it easier to win in 1954.

Marvin Wood didn't exactly follow those same lines of thinking.

"I thought it was a fluke that we made it the first year," Wood says. "We were just a big old county basketball team that had some good bounces that allowed us to get there. We were a young team. Everybody thought, 'We'll be back next year.' That's the way the community looked at it. Everybody in the community felt that way except one person, and I was probably the one person."

Even Gene White thought it was a once-in-a-lifetime chance. "I have to think we thought it was our only chance," he said. "Surely there was enough realism about us to think that."

Engel, the best of the group at remembering in detail, recalls a different set of events.

"After the game, he [Wood] came in and said, 'We came a long way, but I'm going to take the blame for this one. We're going to lose a couple of good ballplayers, and they're going to be missed. Next year, we're going to have it all as far as defense. That's where we got beat here. We will have a tough defense.'

"Nobody had any expectations of going to the Final Four. After we got to the big barn once, we knew we were losing a couple of good boys. But you had to think, 'Wait a minute, we're back to where we were in the sixth grade.' I think it was a burning desire. It was the same guys. It made you say, 'We've got one more chance at this, to get to the big barn one more time.' "

5 *The 1954 Regular Season*

The fifties were a lot different from the nineties. There were no summer camps, no off-season weight training, no AAU tournaments. Nike barely existed, years from hatching its summer camp which brings together the best high school players in the country.

Had Bob Plump grown up in the nineties, he would have spent the summer before his senior year globe-trotting with all-star teams or playing in a McDonald's Classic or making a tour of Europe or displaying his skills for college coaches from New York to Los Angeles. But this was the fifties, and Plump passed his summer like everyone else on his team. He worked. One job was pushing a broom as a janitor for an area business. "It was a boring job," he says. "It was all I could do to stay awake." He also found time to play basketball and have a good time.

Some other Milan players took vacations, but few had the money to go much farther than the next county. Most stayed home. Some players worked, mostly for their parents. All played basketball, either at the school, at Schroders', or at any available barn or driveway goal.

"We just played every chance we got," says Schroder. "We still went to the drive-in movie and played some baseball, but we got the light out and played basketball at night."

"We didn't have a summer program as most schools have it now," said Wood, who passed his summers as a guard at the local Seagrams warehouse. "Our boys just played a lot of basketball in a small community. Pierceville was probably the hot spot. Older boys used to come in there and challenge the younger guys. I think you learn a lot playing against older and more experienced players."

These kids had been competing against older players their entire lives. It came to the point in the summer of 1953 where competition was not easy to find. After all, who wanted to play against a group of kids who had played in the state finals just a few months earlier? Then fall came—and a new season approached.

The team had lost only Jim Call, Ralph Preble, and Jim Wendelman. Replacing Wendelman would be the big challenge for Wood. Gene White was a capable replacement, but he was two inches shorter. Bob Wichman, Rollin Cutter, and Wendelman's younger brother, Ken, would provide help, but it was doubtful that any of those three could completely fill the void.

The other positions seemed solid. Plump and Ray Craft formed one of the best backcourts in Indiana. Bob Engel was sure to be a workhorse at forward, with both points and rebounds, after spending most of 1953 teaming with Plump at guard. Ron Truitt was impressive as a junior on both offense and defense. Throw in Roger Schroder, Bill Jordan, and Glenn Butte, and it was a promising team.

Some others thought otherwise: it could have been a team that was lucky once and now was about to receive a quick dose of reality.

"The so-called experts would have called '53 a fluke," says Schroder. "They would say those guys were lucky. They probably thought that maybe we'd win the regional or maybe we might not even get past Aurora. That was probably a realistic approach. I could see where that would have made sense to some folks."

Recalls White, "We came in with confidence but nobody said, 'Let's go back to state this year.' I really don't recall any pressure

61

at all. We just played the games one at a time. There was optimism. Playing in '53 convinced us we could play with everybody. It gave us the confidence that we didn't have before.''

Plump thinks "we were probably better in '54. We had a little more versatility. . . . We could do more things. I think more teams probably pointed to us, but I don't remember pressure. I don't recall thinking any differently.''

The community was still buzzing about the 1953 tourney and looking toward the sequel. This had been a summer of expectations, of dreaming of a return trip to the big barn. The previous season, great as it had been, was in the books. History. It was time to look ahead again, in the town that now has spent forty years looking back. Getting there in '53 was nice, but winning would be better.

"We all had that feeling they would go back in '54," said White's mother, Genevieve. "There wasn't anybody that didn't think they would go back.''

There was actually one person: Wood. He had warned against overconfidence after the '53 state finals. Now he began to see that complacency of being near the top start to sink in with his supporters. "The season was something they had been waiting on since the '53 tournament,'' Wood said. "Everybody in the community believed we were going back, and many believed we were going to win.

"The greatest doubter in the community was the coach. The coach realized a lot of good things had to happen. Other teams had improved, too.''

That the coach was still there was something of a surprise. Many people thought the young coach might bolt Milan for bigger pastures after his success and sudden fame. Wood's market value obviously had soared. He had taken a virtually anonymous team and had led it to the Final Four.

Milan people also realized Wood's value. They had tried to shower him with monetary and material gifts after the '53 season, but IHSAA rules prohibited that. One gift, however, did slip through. Wood returned home one day to find a new washer and dryer installed in his house. To this day, he claims he has no idea how the appliances got there.

It wasn't because of the new washer and dryer, but Wood didn't leave Milan. He's honest about why. "I thought about it,''

Wood says. "I didn't have the opportunities that year. I didn't go out and search for them."

Wood returned, but Principal Richard Brollier didn't, because of that state tournament ticket hassle. He resigned at the end of the school year. Wood said, "The tickets just got away from him. I think it was the main thing that contributed to his leaving. He had a good rapport with the students. People just got hostile over the tickets."

Longtime school secretary Betty Dobson recalls, "We were all overwhelmed. The townspeople just didn't think he handled it well. He almost had a nervous breakdown over the whole situation."

Emboldened, maybe, by young Marvin Wood's success, the Milan School Board went with youth again, choosing twenty-five-year-old Cale Hudson to replace Brollier. A headline later in the season read, "Babes in Wonderland: Everyone's Young in Milan."

The community did have one experienced man at work in Bob Peak, the self-proclaimed president of the mythical Downtown Coaches Club. He continued his daily visits to Wood's house, to give advice, rehash the previous year's successful season, or just talk about the new year's personnel.

"He was operating," says Wood. "He didn't miss a trick and he didn't miss a day. He was always out promoting Milan basketball. He knew we were going to win the state. He knew before we even opened practice. I didn't consider it putting pressure on the coach. I didn't consider it putting pressure on the team. Knowing Peak, I just considered it good, loyal support. They had a thing going around town that Marv had a bag of tricks. Every time we played somebody big, they expected some new trick to come out of the bag. They kept asking what new tricks we had in the bag for this year. We didn't have any new tricks. We just refined what we had from last year."

Wood conducted what he called a "normal" practice on October 1, the first day allowed under IHSAA guidelines. That was more than two weeks earlier than under the present rules, and made for a six-month season since the state tournament ended the last week of March. The numbers were down considerably from the previous October, when fifty-nine boys had competed for a spot on the team. Just twenty-seven tried out for the 1953–

54 squad. One reason was that every person in town knew who would play on this team.

"When a new coach comes into town, everybody comes out for basketball if they have any ability at all," said Wood. "We had nine players coming back from the '53 team and had an excellent junior varsity team. We had excellent prospects coming up. We didn't have great numbers, but we had quality in what we had."

The Indians also had a new "home" gymnasium—in Versailles, a ten-minute drive south. With their success in '53, the Indians had outgrown their tiny home gym and now opted to play their '54 home games in Versailles' state-of-the-art, in-ground fieldhouse that seated about 3,000 people. It was the architectural forerunner of New Castle's huge fieldhouse, opened in the 1959–60 season and still the largest high school fieldhouse in the world.

Wood held most team practices at the old gym, and he returned to the basics. He was young, but he did know that the team needed to come down to earth a little bit. He knew that six months made for a long season. He knew that just repeating that sectional title would be difficult.

"We went back to the fundamentals," he said. "I told the guys that I didn't think you could forget so many things in such a short period of time. We had to work on defensive stance. We had to work on putting the ball down with the hand away from the defense on the dribble. I've always been a coach who believes the good teams do the little things right."

It would also not be a season in which Milan could surprise anyone. Those days were over, the times when bigger opposing teams thought showing up was good enough for victory.

Milan's success also had other teams wanting to play the Indians. The 1954 schedule looked like one a Muncie Central or a Terre Haute Gerstmeyer might play, not one designed for tiny Milan. Added to what was already a competitive schedule the previous season were Seymour, Frankfort, and Columbus, schools that dwarfed Milan in enrollment figures.

"We got some pretty big games the next year because teams were willing to play the state finalist team," said Schroder. The schedule looked intimidating on paper, but even Wood remained confident about his team's prospects.

"Everyone wanted to come to see and play Milan," Wood said.

"We played before packed houses. Everybody had hopes of beating us. Knowing we were going to be better, we scheduled some bigger schools. We had a pretty strong schedule for a small school. Our guys had a quiet confidence about them. They knew they were good and that it was going to take a good team to beat them. Bigger schools have the opinion that they should beat the smaller schools."

They learned in '54 that wasn't always the case.

Milan opened the campaign with an easy 52–36 victory over Sunman and followed with a 64–41 win against Vevay. Osgood gave the Indians a scare, but Milan pulled out a 44–40 victory for a 3–0 record heading into an early-season showdown with Seymour.

Wood thought his team had been shaky at best. Sunman, Vevay, and Osgood were teams that Milan should have destroyed on paper, but a phenomenon was developing: Every team, no matter how large or small, was inspired to play its best basketball against Milan. Every team wanted to beat the suddenly renowned small-town wonders.

Seymour was the first real test. Beat this bigger school on its own court and everything else should fall into place.

The game was never close. Milan jumped to an early lead and ran away with a 61–43 victory, paced by eighteen points from Craft and fifteen from Plump.

"Seymour just had a huge gym," said Wood. "When we went over there, I knew it was going to be a battle. They had a lot of veterans but they weren't in our class. Actually, the game wasn't even that close. I knew then that we were pretty good and that we could play a lot of teams."

By this time in the season, Wood had his routine set in stone. He worked on defense Monday and Tuesday and followed with offense on Wednesday and Thursday. He devised what he called a "master game plan with a couple of options." Since the team played its home games at Versailles, it boarded a bus late every Friday and Saturday afternoon. The varsity dressed after the third quarter of the junior varsity game, and Wood didn't make his appearance in the locker room until just two minutes remained in the preliminary game. He gave a short talk, assistant coach Clarence Kelly told a joke, and then someone said what amounted to a pre-game prayer.

"We had a moment of silence before games," says Wood. "I'm not sure when it started. One time someone said, 'Why don't we have a moment of silence?' I asked if it was kind of like a prayer and he said yes. I said, 'What do you want to ask for?' These are the things we came up with—the game be played fair and free from injury, and may the best team that night be the winner."

Milan continued to roll after defeating Seymour. The Indians edged Brookville, 24–20, routed Hanover, 67–36, and then held off Lawrenceburg, 50–41. They got past Versailles, 39–35, in a game played at the home gymnasium of both teams. That ran Milan's record to a perfect 8–0 and a No. 18 ranking in the weekly poll heading into what looked to be the toughest two-game stretch of the season—a holiday tourney that featured Frankfort and Columbus, two of the top teams in the state.

But before the Indians could play in the holiday tourney, they suffered their first loss—in practice.

Craft brought the ball upcourt during a scrimmage and passed to Engel, who was cutting across the foul line. Engel faked a jumper and tried a left-handed hook shot. Butte caught him in the air. "When I came down, I didn't land on both feet," said Engel. "I felt something move, but I didn't pay much attention to it. The next morning I could hardly get out of bed." He had suffered the back injury that would limit his playing time the rest of the year—even in the historic championship game.

Engel's injury shifted responsibilities on the Milan team. It was usually a given that Plump would score his points, but White, Truitt, and Craft would need to pick up some of the slack. With Engel on the bench for long stretches, the Indians would look to Cutter and Butte to move their games up a notch. "I knew I would play a bigger role," says Butte. "I didn't feel any pressure. We were oblivious to pressure. Pressure is a journalist's word. I don't think we ever had pressure. I don't think we knew what it was."

Whatever the outcome, it was one of those unavoidable situations that every coach hates to encounter early in the season. If there was any positive aspect of Engel's injury, it was that this Milan team had more than enough talent to take the challenge.

It was also about this time when Bob Collins of the Indianapolis *Star* began to get on Milan's bandwagon. In a column entitled "Milan's Mighty Mites Tougher," he wrote:

Every so often a real little guy muscles into the state high school tourney hoop-de-do, accompanied always by a large ka-zazz from press, fans and officialdom. Sometimes he simply reaches up and smites a big shot, sometimes he even scoots to the semifinals and sometimes, like Milan, he arrives, unexpected but not unwelcome, at Butler's Fieldhouse door as an accredited member of the Final Four. Traditionally, the little guy, after the usual pre-season fanfare, drops back among the agate scores to dream of things past and wait, hopefully, for one more opportunity. This trip, however, Marvin Wood and the Mighty Men of Milan refuse to be discarded. The Redskins have conked everyone in sight and reports from the southeast say they are capable of handling one and all, large or small.

Most people realized that Milan could not complete the regular season with an unblemished record. Only the real dreamers, or optimists, thought the Indians could turn in a 21–0 season. It ended at eight when Frankfort nailed Milan in the Columbus holiday tourney, 49–47.

The biggest character test came later that night in the consolation game. How Milan would bounce back against an equally tough Columbus team might signal just how much success it would have later in the season. Columbus lost a close afternoon game to top-ranked Fort Wayne North and then practiced before the evening match-up with Milan. The game was close, but the Indians responded well with a 52–49 victory behind Plump's seventeen points.

That split in the holiday tourney put the Indians 9–1 at the halfway mark, with a lot of confidence and many obstacles between them and a spot back in the big barn. That one loss—and the few close games—had brought out some of the skeptics. They said Milan had begun the slide so customary for small schools after a successful season.

"You lose and people say that's right, they aren't as good as they say they are," said Craft. "Then you're back to square one."

Overlooked was that Milan had lost just once in ten games, despite not having a real home gymnasium. The Indians had played just once in the Milan gym, the 67–36 victory over Hanover. The remaining home games had been played at Versailles. The Milan fans didn't mind the short drive, and the players and coaches found that the gym was really just a home away from home.

"We played so many games over there that it was just like being in the home gym," said Schroder.

Plump recalls, "I liked the Versailles floor. It was bigger and it worked to our advantage. It opened up more opportunities."

"We were tough in our home gym," says Wood. "Fans were right up on the court. The walls were two or three feet from the court. There was three feet from the stage and the bleachers to the court. You get to the point where you can shoot with your eyes shut."

The second half of the season began with a 74–60 win over Rising Sun that sent Milan into the Ripley County Tournament on a positive note. This tourney was important to the two-time defending champion Indians. First, this event still carried bragging rights in their home county. Second, there was "Vic." A third consecutive title would give Milan permanent possession of the traveling trophy that went to the winner of each year's tourney. The state trip had given Milan an aura. There was a chance that decisive wins might demoralize the county teams and make winning the sectional a little bit easier.

The games were close, but the Indians won their third straight crown, thanks largely to Plump. He scored twenty-eight points in an opening 52–46 win over Versailles and followed with twenty points in a 44–30 triumph over Holton. White took scoring honors in the finals, with fourteen points in a 36–30 victory against Napoleon.

Seven games remained, but it might have been better for all concerned to fast-forward to the Versailles Sectional.

Milan won six of those last seven games—over Hanover (38–33), Napoleon (61–29), Sunman (42–36), Versailles (49–42), North Vernon (38–37), and Osgood (38–30). The once-beaten Indians were ranked thirteenth, their highest spot ever, when they met old rival Aurora and lost, 54–45. They dropped out of the rankings after the loss.

"Mr. Wood said he didn't pay much attention to the ratings," said Engel. "The other team may have a better record. They may be better, but they have to prove it when they step out there between the hoops. Those are the proving grounds. We never did think we were unbeatable. Aurora beat us and Frankfort beat us in the holiday tourney. We knew we could be beaten. Every step that we took, we corrected what had taken us by the wayside."

Most of the players say they did not look past any regular-season games. "When you have that roundball, you wanted to go on forever," said Engel. "There was no rush for anything. You just wanted to play, play, play."

But in retrospect, it seems one of two things happened in the 1954 regular season. Either Milan was indeed looking to the tourney, or its opponents were stronger and a lot more determined. The average margin of victory for the Indians was more than eighteen points in 1953. It shrank to just under ten points in 1954. And the 1954 team was supposed to be more experienced and more talented.

"I think maybe we took a lot of the season for granted," said Wood. "Many times we were just going through the motions— just getting on with the season and bringing on the tournament. We could not beat a county team by more than ten or twelve points. We struggled against a lot of teams we should have blown out. We didn't hold back anything. We had to use everything we had. I thought maybe our guys were putting some pressure on themselves to blow those teams out. They were a little tense. We won but we struggled."

That was never more evident than in the last regular-season game against Osgood. The Indians, coming off the loss at Aurora, edged Osgood, 38–30. An enraged Wood knew a performance like that would not even get Milan past the sectional, let alone back to the big barn.

"He told us no basketball the week before the sectional," says White. "He didn't want us touching the basketball. I didn't pick up a basketball until Wednesday night before we played on Thursday. He detected some fatigue."

All things considered, it was not a good way for the Indians to head into the state tournament.

• • •

Muncie Central coach Jay McCreary pulled a similar stunt after his team's next-to-last regular-season contest. The Bearcats had virtually given away a 49–45 game to Frankfort, the team that had beaten Milan earlier in the season. The loss dropped Muncie Central to a 14–5 record and out of contention for the top spot in the weekly poll. It also had damaged hopes for another North Central Conference title. Now the team had to defeat

Marion the following weekend and also hope that Logansport could handle Indianapolis Tech. Said McCreary after the loss, "I tried to tell them all week that we weren't going to Frankfort to play against five sticks of stove wood."

"We went over there and played horribly," McCreary remembers. "We had a meeting after the game, and I was the only one who talked. We got outhustled, outshot, outplayed. You could hear me for six miles. I really let them have it."

It must have worked, because Muncie Central returned home to rout Marion 70–48 in the regular-season finale. And Logansport handled Tech to give the Bearcats the NCC crown. That concluded a 15–5 up-and-down season that still had McCreary claiming his team was the best in the state. He told the Muncie *Star*, "I think they are good enough to go just as far in the tournament as any team anyone cares to name. This bunch is good enough for me."

Tournament tradition certainly was on McCreary's side. This was a school that had a chance to win just because of the name across the front of its purple and white jerseys. In the past three seasons, the Bearcats had compiled a combined record of 74–12 and won two state championships. Only four teams outside the tough North Central Conference had managed to defeat a Bearcat squad.

So it was no surprise that many people in addition to the ever-optimistic McCreary picked Muncie Central to add another state crown.

"I thought I had the ballclub to win the state," said McCreary. "I had size, speed, savvy, and we were tough. I had a ballclub that was big. I thought we would go with that."

The local papers touted Muncie Central's 1953–54 squad as the tallest in school history and one of the tallest in the state. Wrote Bill Terhune in the Muncie *Evening Press* the night before the season opener, "Year in and out Central's Bearcats and a few other top-flight contenders provoke a flurry of apprehensive glances from far and near when they begin making their field goals. It's understandable. When you're on top—or near it—everyone begins measuring you for the role of the vanquished. When you're down, nobody cares one way or the other."

Dale Burgess of the Associated Press wrote in November: "The next Indiana high school basketball champion probably is beginning its season this week. That's a pretty safe statement given a list of starters that includes Logansport at Rochester, South Bend Central's defending champs against Gary Roosevelt, Muncie Central against Winchester, Lafayette against Lebanon, Ft. Wayne North Side against Indianapolis Attucks and Huntingburg against Washington. It would be safer if Ft. Wayne South Side, the big Evansville clubs and most of the Calumet teams weren't waiting another week to start."

The United Press state poll tabbed Muncie Central as the team to beat for the state championship. One writer even said, "But among the 753 teams eligible to compete for the state title, there surely won't be another Milan to steal headlines from the city teams." McCreary made no predictions on the eve of the season. "You can be assured," he told the local papers, "that we will show up for the games."

So the Bearcats headed into their opener with Winchester, knowing the town—and the state—expected nothing less than a trip to the Final Four. The school sold more than 7,000 adult and student season tickets to guarantee a sell-out for the entire season. The campaign started promisingly enough with an 81–33 thumping of Winchester. It disintegrated quickly. A one-point loss at Shelbyville followed the next weekend and was punctuated by the arrest of four Muncie youths at the Shelbyville Youth Recreation Center during a post-game dance. Everyone involved compared the Shelbyville victory to David over Goliath, and the police attributed the violence and arrests to the fact that "Muncie Central lost a ballgame."

The season got worse before it got better. The one-point Shelbyville loss was followed by a 53–43 thumping by top-ranked Fort Wayne North before the hometown fans. Said McCreary after the game, "We're pretty far down right now, but we're far from out."

The coach called a practice for the next day and began to make some major changes. He realized height was not enough, that he needed to complement some of it with quickness. He realized he needed to start virtually from scratch. "I found out after the third game that we had trouble just getting the ball up the floor," he says now. "It was just an entire revamp of the system."

There were really two major changes—sophomore guards Jimmy Barnes and Phil Raisor replaced two upperclassmen in

71

the starting lineup. Barnes would be forever linked with Milan and the 1954 state tournament later that year, but for now he concentrated solely on changing the fortunes of a 1–2 team.

The season turned around quickly for the Bearcats. They put together a six-game winning streak before falling to Fort Wayne South in a holiday tourney. They won seven of the next eight before the debacle at Frankfort.

With the season-ending rout of Marion, there was no doubt that Muncie Central was a legitimate contender to win the state title.

But for those who believed in omens, there was one on the horizon. The victory over Marion had given Muncie Central its third North Central Conference title in five years. It had lost in the tournament each of those seasons. In contrast, the Bearcat squad that had finished second in the NCC in 1951 and 1952 had gone on to win the state crown.

At that moment, however, McCreary felt nothing but confidence heading into the 1954 title chase.

• • •

As Milan prepared to make its second improbable run, the Versailles *Republican* again ran a tribute to the team from the cheerleaders. It was simple, yet it showed the emphasis on basketball, the tournament, and how much these players meant to a school and community.

It's easy to laugh at by today's standards. Enviable, though, is a simpler time when basketball was indeed king and nothing else mattered but the games.

> We, cheerleaders, and all of the fans at Milan couldn't be any prouder of our Indian team. We are glad to have the privilege of introducing them to you fans.
>
> Gene White is a senior and is on the starting five for his second year. His position is center and forward. He is a proficient rebounder and an artist at tip-ins and set shots.
>
> Bob Engel is a senior and plays forward. This is his third year on the starting five and we think he is one of the best long and jump shots in Southeastern Indiana. We are happy to have Bob back in the starting lineup since he had to limit his actions favoring his injured back.

Ronnie Truitt, another senior, and forward is returning to the first five for his second year. He is an excellent rebounder and set shot.

Bob Plump is a senior and plays guard. . . . He is known throughout the state for his excellent driving ability and jump shots.

Ray Craft, another senior, is one of the finest and fastest guards in Southeastern Indiana. He is an excellent driver and set shot man.

Kenny Wendelman is a senior and a returning letter man. He plays center and forward. He is a fine rebounder, a fast man on the defense and a good shot.

Roger Schroder is another senior and letter man. He is a fine shot and a good ball handler and a defensive man. His position is guard.

Bill Jordan is a junior and is also a letter man. He plays forward. He is a good rebounder and set shot man.

Bob Wichman is our other junior. He joined MHS at the beginning of the year from Kansas. He plays center and is an excellent rebound man. He also has a beautiful hook shot.

Glenn Butte is a sophomore and a fine up-and-coming star. His position is forward and he is excellent in all phases of the sport.

Rollin Cutter is also a sophomore and plays center and guard. He is an excellent ballhandler, set shot and rebounder. He is bound to be one of our future stars.

Coach Marvin Wood, we think, is superb to say the least. He has displayed excellent ability in guiding and securing the utmost performance of his talented and successful team. His untiring efforts merit the high esteem of his boys and loyal fans.

Our assistant coaches, Marc Combs and Clarence Kelly, are to be congratulated for their untiring efforts.

Our student managers, Fred Busching and Oliver Jones, deserve much credit for their hard work, cooperation and dependability.

We are proud also to say that we have Vic to keep for the third consecutive year and we are honored to be the cheerleaders for the Milan Indians.

May the best team win!
Pat Bohlke
Marjorie Ent
Virginia Voss

6 *The 1954 Tournament*

The pep session that sent Milan into the sectional followed along the lines of previous rallies until the last speaker took the microphone. It was local resident Freda Whitlach, the architect of the town's 100th-anniversary celebration. She was writing a book for the event and told the assembled throng that she would wait until after the state tournament to pen the conclusion. "She hoped we were starting along the trail that would be very special and important in the script," says Marvin Wood. "That just added a little more incentive."

Until that time, no one had really thought much about the connection between the town's birthday and basketball. Now it started to make a little bit of sense. Maybe it was fate that Milan had lost in the afternoon game of the '53 state finals. It wouldn't sound nearly as impressive in the nineties had Milan won the state basketball title in its ninety-ninth year. One hundred. The centennial. The nice, round number.

A few weeks before that pep session, the Indianapolis *Star Magazine* ran a one-page photo spread on Milan's "Hoop Happy

Hoosiers." Part of the text read, "The boys still are playing big-time basketball in the small, but enthusiastic community of Milan in Ripley County. Milan High School's Indians, finalists in last year's state tournament, again are sharpening their tomahawks. They may not travel so far this year, largely because there is no tendency to underestimate their ability. But Milan citizens are convinced that the boys will do themselves proud."

Wood knew that what most of the citizens meant by "proud" involved another trip to the state finals. "We had been fortunate the previous year," Wood said. "One of the goals the young men established then was to make it back to the Fieldhouse. I was probably the most nervous person in the community. It would have been extremely embarrassing to me had we lost in the sectional tournament. You can have bad games, you can have terrible games. I thought we were ready. I knew the young men were focused on the tournament."

Says Craft, "I'm sure the people expected us to win the sectional. If somebody had asked me, I would have said that I expected us to win it."

Says Engel, "We had a good ballclub, and we knew it was going to take a good ballclub to beat us."

The mandatory break from basketball Wood had ordered evidently helped. Milan had no trouble in the sectional opener, winning 83–36 over Cross Plains. All ten players scored, and Bill Jordan was the leader with fifteen points. The other games were closer, but there wasn't really a scare. The Indians downed Versailles, 57–43, in the semifinals and then defeated Osgood, 44–32, for the championship.

Those three victories were all that Wood needed to see.

"After the sectional," Wood says, "I went home and told my wife this is what they had been waiting on—the tournament. I knew we were ready. We cruised in the sectional. The biggest concern I had was that we didn't peak too early."

Milan was on a roll again. And the Indians couldn't have picked a better time, because three solid opponents—Aurora, Rushville, and Connersville—awaited in the regional. Milan drew host Rushville in the opener, with the Spartans and Red Devils to meet in the second game. Rushville would be dangerous because of the home crowd, Aurora had already defeated Milan earlier in the season, and Connersville would be looking for revenge after the loss in the previous year's regional final.

Rushville came into the regional with an unimpressive 11–12 record. Records don't matter much in the tournament, but the featured game matched Aurora (20–2) and Connersville (19–4).

The records didn't lie. Milan, which arrived at the regional in the traditional new Pontiacs provided by car dealer Chris Volz, had little trouble in a 58–34 rout, behind a game-high sixteen points from Plump. Aurora's Bob Fehrman helped make easy work of Connersville in the second game. He scored a regional-record thirty-five points that keyed the Red Devils' 67–51 victory.

That set up the game that the area had awaited for three weeks. Milan versus Aurora. The defending regional champions and state finalists against the perennial power that had handed the Indians one of only two losses in the regular season. The team that advanced to the semistate would know it had beaten the best to get there.

Few contests in sports live up to expectations. This one did. "That was probably the most aggressive crowd I have ever seen at a basketball game," says Wood. "The crowds were there more than an hour before the game, and the teams weren't even there yet. When we walked in the gym, our crowd said, 'Best team is in the black.' The Aurora crowd said, 'Best team is in the white.' "

That was just the crowd. Wood especially didn't like what he saw when he looked at the Aurora team. "Aurora was intimidating," he said. "I was concerned if we could get the job done. The teams were traditional rivals. The communities didn't like each other, and the main reason was basketball."

One of the big keys for Milan would be how well it controlled Fehrman. White drew the assignment. The flip side of that coin would be how well Aurora defended Plump. Fehrman had scored twenty-three points and Plump twelve in the regular-season matchup.

Both teams wanted to start quickly to quiet the other team's crowd. Milan took a 6–1 lead, but Aurora fought back to tie the game at 13 after the first quarter. The Red Devils took over in the second period, turning a 19–18 advantage into a 27–20 halftime lead.

Perhaps more than at any other time in the entire tournament, it seemed that Milan might be finished. Aurora had the momentum and a seven-point lead. It also had the confidence of knowing it had defeated Milan earlier in the season. More than even that, Engel had a bad back and three fouls, and Truitt had collected two fouls. The Indians needed those two in the lineup to have any chance at all in the second half.

"I thought Aurora had the best talent of anybody we played," said Plump. "I remember sitting in the locker room at the half and thinking, 'Oh no, it's not going to end now?' There were seeds of doubt in my mind at that time."

Aurora still led 34–28 heading into the fourth quarter. To compound troubles, Truitt had picked up his fourth foul. With just eight minutes remaining in the regional final, it looked like the best team was in the white.

The Indians needed a hero, a savior, in that fourth quarter. The entire team took the challenge.

After a field goal from Craft and a free throw each from Plump and White, Truitt hit a corner jumper to tie the game at 34. After two Aurora free throws, Truitt hit another jumper and Craft added a free throw to give Milan a 37–36 lead. Plump hit another free throw for 38–36, Engel an outside jumper for 40–36.

Out came the cat-and-mouse game. Engel, White, and Plump all hit shots in the next two minutes to put the game out of reach at 46–36.

"We had the little spurt and caught them in the last quarter," said Wood. "They died and their crowd died."

The game ended a minute later at 46–38. Milan had put together its most impressive quarter of the season when it needed it most, outscoring the Red Devils 18–4. Engel, bad back and all, scored seventeen points. White turned in a defensive gem, holding Fehrman to just twelve points.

"A lot of people didn't think we were going to come back," says Engel. "I never had that feeling. You're never beaten until it's over. I know that sounds crazy, but there's that drive behind you. I thought, 'We've got another quarter to go.' Our skin just got tougher as far as pressure."

Says Cutter, "It was a pretty game. Things just seemed to work out for us. I think it was partly confidence and a lot of preparation, emotionally and psychologically. Woody was great at that."

Says Plump, "I don't remember being concerned in another game."

Bunny Shot of the Cincinnati *Enquirer* was back on Milan's bandwagon. He wrote, "You'll have to go a long way to see better basketball than was played at Rushville Saturday. And nowhere have we seen a team with more aggressive spirit, poise and drive than the Milan Indians which won the tourney. Even when Marvin Wood's boys were trailing Aurora—a team well worthy of going to the state—they still played their own game. And woe be unto the team that lets Milan get a substantial lead. Such a quintet will have plenty of trouble even getting its hands on the ball."

Aurora, even in defeat, returned home to a huge parade. Milan chose to postpone its celebration. "The crowd wanted to celebrate but the coach wouldn't let them," said Wood. "We had set a standard: as long as we were in the tournament, we were not going to celebrate. We went back to Milan and went home."

Says Engel, "We didn't go crazy. There was nothing elaborate. We had to say, 'Wait a minute. We've got a few more to go.' "

The school held a brief pep session on the Monday afternoon following the regional, and then things proceeded as usual. Wood taught biology, health, and physical education during the day at Milan. Or at least he tried. "We would like to think there was school but there was not really," says Wood. "All of the attention of everybody was on basketball. We had classes every day. We had students who would try to get me off onto basketball, and it wasn't difficult to do."

Much like the previous year, people in the region wanted to know more about this tiny town beginning to earn headlines across the country. The society columnist for the Cincinnati *Post* obliged with a feature entitled "We Learn about Milan-tics." He wrote:

> In Milan to see the reaction to the regional triumph Monday and had quite a day. Folks were working, but not very hard, while others were frankly loafing and enjoying re-hash of the regional.
>
> Ate with Lou Kirschner (a Sunman transplant) and Earl Voss, who knew how to find Montezuma on the road map. Good food at Arkenberg's, too. They knew we were coming but we didn't see any cake.
>
> Over to learn from Bert and Bud Draime that they'd brew us a nickel cup of coffee, and made plans for St. Patrick's Day. Bert told

Milan center Jim Wendelman passes against Shelbyville in the 1953 semistate. Photo courtesy of the Indianapolis *News*/Bill Herman.

Ray Craft goes up for a layup in the 1953 state finals. Photo courtesy of the Indianapolis *Star*/James C. Ramsey.

The team prepares to leave for Indianapolis and the 1953 state finals.

1953–54 team photo. *Front row, from left to right:* Ray Craft, Bill Jordan, Gene White, Bob Plump, Roger Schroder. *Back row, from left to right:* Ken Wendelman, Bob Wichman, Ron Truitt, Glenn Butte, Bob Engel, Rollin Cutter.

Coach Marvin Wood instructs the team during a 1954 practice.

Milan classroom. *First row, front to back:* Jim Nichols, Joanne Steinmetz, David Jeffries. *Second row:* Anita Womack, Bob Plump, Roger Schroder. *Third row:* Pat Busteed, Carl Richardson, Virginia Voss, Gene White.

The Milan starting five. *From left to right:* Ray Craft, Ron Truitt, Bob Engel, Gene White, Bob Plump. Photo courtesy of the Indianapolis *News*/Bill Doeppers.

Milan captains Bob Plump (*left*) and Gene White meet with the Aurora captains before the Milan-Aurora regional final in 1954 in the Rushville gymnasium.

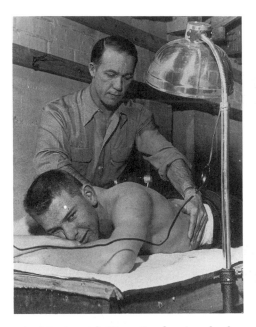

Assistant coach Marc Combs gives back treatment to Milan forward Bob Engel. Photo courtesy of the Indianapolis *News*/Bill Doeppers.

Coach Wood cuts down the net after the 1954 semistate victory. Photo courtesy of Platt Photo, Columbus, Indiana.

Ray Craft works on the family farm.
Photo courtesy of the *Indiana Farmer's
Guide*, Huntington, Indiana.

Gene White works at his father's feed
store. Photo courtesy of the *Indiana
Farmer's Guide*, Huntington, Indiana.

Ron Truitt (*left*) and Bob Engel work at Chris Volz Chevrolet. Photo courtesy of
the *Indiana Farmer's Guide*, Huntington, Indiana.

Mary Lou Wood and her two children.

Milan's Ray Craft and Ron Truitt battle Terre Haute Gerstmeyer's Arley Andrews for a loose ball in the afternoon game of the 1954 state finals. Photo courtesy of the Indianapolis *Star*/ Frank H. Fisse.

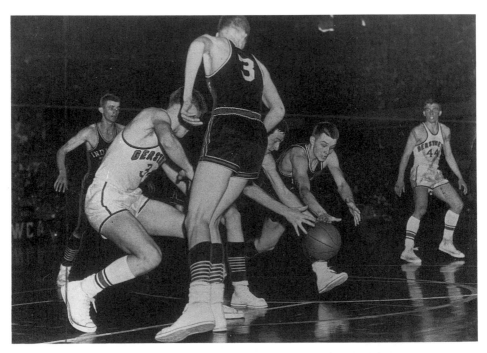

Ray Craft and Gene White fight for a loose ball against Terre Haute Gerstmeyer. Photo courtesy of the Indianapolis *Star*/Frank H. Fisse.

Milan cheerblock at the 1954 state finals.

Milan's Ray Craft tries a layup against Muncie Central's Jim Hinds. Photo courtesy of the Indianapolis *Star*/Maurice Burnett.

Milan fans at the 1954 state finals.

Milan's Bob Plump goes up against Muncie Central's Jim Hinds and Robert Crawford (10). Photo courtesy of the Indianapolis *Star*/James C. Ramsey.

Milan students cheer on their team at the 1954 state finals.

Milan fans at the 1954 state finals.

Bill Jordan hugs coach Marvin Wood as Bob Plump hits the last-second shot to win the game. Photo courtesy of the Indianapolis *Star*/Robert J. Shaffer.

Muncie Central after the last-second shot by Plump. *From left to right:* Jimmy Barnes, Phil Raisor, Leon Aguillana, John Casterlow, John Flowers; *in back:* principal Loren Chastain, assistant coach Carl Adams, assistant coach Don Markle, Jim Hinds. Photo courtesy of the Indianapolis *Star*/James C. Ramsey.

Milan students after the victory.

Milan center Gene White hugs cheerleader Patty Bohlke after the championship game. Photo courtesy of the Indianapolis *Star*/ Robert J. Shaffer.

Bob Plump cuts down the net.

Milan residents celebrate the victory. Photo courtesy of the Indianapolis *News*/ Bill Herman.

A Greensburg resident greets the caravan on its way back to Milan.

A crowd greets the caravan as it passes through Sunman. Photo courtesy of the Indianapolis *News*/ Bill Herman.

Color guard leads a parade in Sunman on the day following the victory.
Photo courtesy of the Indianapolis *News*/William Palmer.

Motorcade into Milan on the day following the victory. Photo courtesy of the
Indianapolis *News*/William Palmer.

Milan team with trophy. *From left to right:* Ken Wendelman, Gene White, Bob Engel, Roger Schroder, Ray Craft, Bob Plump, Ron Truitt.

Banquet for the players following their victory in the state tournament.

Indiana All-Stars (*left to right*) Milan's Bob Plump, Elkhart's Ray Ball, Jeffersonville's Pete Obrensky, Mississinewa's Larry Headen, Terre Haute Gerstmeyer's Arley Andrews.

Milan's town marker and greeting board. Photo courtesy of Ron Tower.

The water tower painted to commemorate the championship team. Photo courtesy of Ron Tower.

The championship trophy in the lobby of the Milan gymnasium. Photo courtesy of Ron Tower.

us of a good trombone man, the new country club manager, and we forgot his name.

Jim Laws and I outmatched Bill Steinmetz for coffee at the drug store and between basketball conversation, Jim told us of some undertakings (he's a funeral director) in the hills of neighboring Hazard, Ky. Interesting, too.

Postmaster C. R. Nagel told us his son will go into service, won't play Tri-County league baseball this year. Virgil (Red) Smith came across the street to squint through our Polaroid. Attorney Bob Peak stopped by to privately wonder how Milan's win over Aurora would affect his relations with Aurora attorneys. We watched our language with one of the ministers.

Best quote of the day was Peck Truitt's: We took the roar out of Aurora, now let's take the zoom out of Montezuma.

Coach Marvin Wood was in Morrell's, waiting to pick up the tape recording of the regional for use at school. Woody waited until the entire record had been played for the fans outside, just another example of the swell type fellow he is.

At the school, we choked out a few hundred well-chosen words, unaccustomed as we are. Explained our private regional jinx that brings the crown to the Versailles sectional winner (four in a row). Reminded the youngsters that in 1930 their gym was the site of a 14-team sectional tourney, was considered the latest thing.

To put us in our place, Indians Ron Truitt and Bob Engel barked our nose by calling our attention to a slipped bow tie that hadn't slipped.

Get out the Cadillacs, Chris, those boys might be going back.

We like it in Milan.

Milan and Terre Haute Gerstmeyer, playing in the Bloomington Semistate, were the only two '53 Final Four teams to reach the '54 Sweet Sixteen. South Bend Central, the '53 champion, lost to Elkhart in the regional. Richmond fell to tiny Milton in its own sectional. The turnover was not unusual. In eighteen years, only seven teams had won back-to-back semistate crowns.

The Indianapolis Semistate matched Milan (24–2) against Montezuma (23–5) in the first game, Crispus Attucks (23–4) against Columbus (21–5) in the second. Montezuma had beaten two other small schools to win the Greencastle Regional: Fillmore, 55–52, and New Ross, 70–61. Attucks won the always-tough Indianapolis Sectional, then added the regional championship with a 54–44 triumph over Fortville and a 64–48 win against Alexandria. Co-

79

lumbus won at Shelbyville over Greensburg, 72–67, and Scottsburg, 62–50.

The tourney appeared to be wide open on paper. None of the teams had much height—Sheddrick Mitchell of Attucks was the semistate's tallest player at 6-4.

To add a little irony to the occasion, Milan was suddenly the big school in its opening game. Milan had only seventy-five boys enrolled at the time of the 1954 tournament, but Montezuma had just thirty-six. Montezuma also had the crowd favorite in five-foot, 100-pound freshman guard Bill Knoblett, who sometimes had trouble convincing people he was not the team mascot.

Milan's routine was similar to that of the previous season, with one big difference. In 1953, the excited Milan players had combined basketball and fun. Many of them had never been to Indianapolis before the '53 semistate. They won, but it eventually caught up to them the following week in the state finals. In 1954, the players concentrated on winning basketball games. Period. And Wood says he didn't have to say a word about it. The players knew what had happened.

"In '53, if they decorated the cars we were there," says Craft. "The tourney started [in '54], we practiced and we went home. There was no horsing around. We had a job to do."

The Milan team made a brief appearance at a Friday pep session, then headed to Indianapolis in the new Buicks provided by Volz. He was probably already thinking about how he would get the Cadillacs to take the team to the state finals.

Lodging again was at the Pennsylvania Hotel, far from the frenzied atmosphere of Butler Fieldhouse. The team ate its meals—breakfast, lunch, and dinner—at the Apex Grill. Wood also invited Indianapolis policeman Pat Stark back to serve as the team's escort to and from the Fieldhouse. Friday night was uneventful, a good sign that Saturday could be even better.

For the second consecutive weekend, Milan had the luck of playing the first game. That meant the Indians, if they could get past Montezuma, would be relaxing back at the hotel long before the second game was over. When they prepared to leave for the Fieldhouse, Stark made his promise to the players: If they won the state title, he would take them around Monument Circle the *wrong way*. "When he made this promise, they didn't forget it," says Wood.

But that was four games away, a long way in the future. There would be more pressure and more at stake in these four games than in any games in these players' entire lives.

It was an advantage for Milan that it had been in the semistate the year before. Butler Fieldhouse didn't look as intimidating as on that first visit in '53. "Walking into Butler Fieldhouse in '53 was like Hickory walking into Hinkle in the movie," says Craft. "We were amazed at the size of the place. The next year, you've been there. I think the awe was not there because it was the second time around."

Wood already had his game-day plan before the Indians arrived in Indianapolis on Friday night. "We tried to follow the same format for the tournament as we followed for the regular season," he said. "I didn't like to get to the Fieldhouse early. We would plan to get there so we could get ready, have a short briefing and a warmup. Then the game was ready to play. We thought we were ready for anything people would throw at us."

Montezuma, the first team from Parke County ever to play in a semistate, also was ready. Milan led 20–10 after the first quarter and 29–21 at the half. The Indians went to the cat-and-mouse game midway through the third period, but it threatened to backfire. Milan hit only one of six shots in the quarter and went into the fourth quarter leading the Aztecs just 32–30.

The marvel of live television became evident to Wood at about that point. He received a telegram sent to Butler Fieldhouse at 2:26 P.M. that read: "Coach Marvin Wood, Butler Fieldhouse, Watch your out of bounds at far end only one receiver back and him not alert for pressing you must expect fouls inevitable aggressive play but too many of type when odds on benefit are low and odds on foul high." It was signed, "TV fan."

The cat-and-mouse proved more effective in the fourth period. Milan built a 38–31 lead with just over four minutes remaining. That forced Montezuma to foul, and Milan efficiently capitalized for a 44–34 win. There was definitely no time to celebrate the victory. The winner of Attucks and Columbus would be waiting that evening.

Wood and the team watched more than half of the second game, then returned to the Apex Grill for a post-game meal before heading back to the hotel for some rest. They listened to the second half of the Columbus-Attucks game on the radio while they were eating. "We were hoping Columbus would win," says Schroder. "We knew we could beat Columbus."

Columbus probably should have won and had a chance for revenge against Milan, but Attucks overcame a fourteen-point second-half deficit for a 68–67 triumph. Oscar Robertson's free throw with twenty-five seconds remaining won the game.

"Attucks was the unknown as far as we were concerned," says Cutter. "We knew we could play against Columbus because we had beaten them earlier in the year. Then Attucks came back and won. Roger Schroder said, 'Well, guys, we'll just have to beat Attucks tonight.' Everybody heard him. I remember it like he was sitting right here saying it. It was one of those comments that came at the right time, was said by the right person, that just gave you a little confidence because I'm sure that all of us were sitting there saying, 'Now what are we going to do?' "

Looking back, Schroder thinks it was a good omen that Attucks did win that afternoon game.

"I'm sure we would have let down," Schroder says of the potential game with Columbus. "They might have nailed us. Every time you beat somebody, it's harder to beat them the next time. You let down because you've already beaten them. They concentrate a little better and they gear it up a little more."

The game with Attucks was a study in contrasts before it began. Crispus Attucks was an all-black team. The Ku Klux Klan had demonstrated when the school had opened in 1927. The IHSAA didn't allow "colored" schools to play in the state tournament until 1943, and even then few teams were willing to play those schools—Gary Roosevelt, Evansville Lincoln, and Attucks. Milan had ten white players. No blacks lived in the entire town of Milan in '54.

Attucks, which had reached the state for the first time in 1951, had been rolling over foes. At the conclusion of each game, the Attucks fans broke into a rendition of what they called the "Crazy Song." It went something like this:

Oh (————) was rough
Oh (————) was tough
They can beat everybody
But they can't beat us
(Chorus)

Hi de hi de hi de hi
Hi de hi de hi de ho
Oh, skip, bop beat 'em
That's the crazy song . . .

The fat lady sang for Attucks on Saturday night. Maybe Columbus wore Attucks down in the close afternoon contest. Or maybe Milan was just better.

The Indians trailed 17–16 after the first quarter, mainly because Robertson had scored eleven points. "I thought he was super," Plump says. "He was pretty fluid and a heck of a basketball player when he was a sophomore. I'm glad we got him when he was a sophomore and not a senior."

Robertson's turn would come in the future; Plump's time was now. Plump scored his tournament-high twenty-eight points. Milan outscored Attucks 23–15 in the second period to take a 39–32 halftime advantage, and the cat-and-mouse dominated the second half. Attucks cut the lead to 54–47 before Milan used its slowdown game as an offensive weapon. The Indians worked the ball for three consecutive easy field goals—by Engel, Plump, and Truitt—to put the game out of reach at 60–47. Some free throws made the final 65–52, a score that still seems stunning considering Robertson's special greatness and the history he, coach Ray Crowe, and Attucks were to write the next two years: back-to-back state championships, the first unbeaten championship season in history in 1955–56.

The regional victory over Aurora was big because it came against an old foe, but the one over Attucks was the most impressive, then and now. Attucks had a good team and it had Robertson. For Milan to beat the Tigers showed once and for all that this team was for real.

Crowe, who played the white-haired coach of runner-up South Bend in *Hoosiers,* is retired now, with an office in the same complex with Plump on the north side of Indianapolis. They have relived that game on many occasions. "Ray Crowe told me that was the worst defeat that any of his tournament teams ever suffered," says Plump. "When I look back on it, I think it's surprising that we defeated them by as much as we did. They couldn't handle the cat-and-mouse offensively. It was relatively easy after we got ahead. I didn't even know they were rated that high and they were that good. I facetiously tell people that we didn't get news down there until about two weeks after it happened."

Engel remembers the gentlemanly Crowe walking "down to our dressing room after the game. He came over and congratulated every boy. I can see him standing there like it was yesterday. He said, 'You've got the best coach in the business. We have gotten beat every way you could get beaten. When you could get the ball out quick, you went on a fastbreak. You outran us. You outrebounded us. You outscored us. You did everything right.' "

"The 'blues' replaced the Attucks 'crazy song' on Indiana Ave. last night," the Indianapolis *Star* reported Sunday. "Most of the people seemed stunned as though they couldn't realize what happened. A man at the Cooks and Waiters Club, 337 Indiana Ave., said, 'Aw, man, I heard the final score. I feel awful.' "

By this time, almost everyone had jumped on the Milan bandwagon, including most of the supposedly impartial sportswriters. Three-hundred-pound Tiny Hunt, the sports editor for the Versailles *Republican,* was the ringleader. Bunny Shot of the Cincinnati *Post* ran a close second. Shot wrote after the win over Attucks, "Sat next to a reporter from Danville, Ill., in the press box. He was following Montezuma. During the night game, he lost his voice, right with Bunny Shot, cheering for Bob Plump, Ray Craft and the other Indians when they were cat-and-mousing the Tigers. 'Never saw two better players,' he yelled in our ear. Bunny was so nervous after watching the rebounding of Attucks in the afternoon that we got a touch of indigestion after dinner and remarked to a well-known chunky feller who answers to the name of 'Tiny' that we were afraid Milan wouldn't be able to get enough rebounds to win at night. Gene White, Ron Truitt and Engel took care of that—and how! He didn't have any voice left either to say, 'I told you so.' "

The Milan players became the instant darlings of the state for the second consecutive March. Very few people outside Ripley County had actually thought that the Indians would make it back for another shot at the title. Now, everyone wanted to jump on the fast-moving bandwagon. The biggest task for Wood was to keep his team focused on the games. He again postponed any celebrations, saying much more basketball remained. He tried to deflect as many questions as possible from the players to himself. Under no circumstances would there be a repeat of 1953, when the players had become so enthralled by being in the state finals that they forgot to concentrate on the opponent.

The three other state finalists in '54, on paper at least, had legitimate chances to win the title. Elkhart had survived in the Lafayette Semistate, Muncie Central at Fort Wayne, and Terre Haute Gerstmeyer at Bloomington. Each school came into the finals on an incredible high, and each school also had a story to tell.

Gerstmeyer didn't want to be a bridesmaid for the second straight March. The Black Cats had barely missed in '53, losing the final game to South Bend Central, 42–41. Their city had never won a state title, and this looked like one of their best teams ever. Gerstmeyer still had two of its future Hall of Famers, Arley Andrews and "Uncle" Harold Andrews, plus Hall of Fame–bound coach Howard Sharpe.

Gerstmeyer was 31–2 on a schedule that included East Chicago Roosevelt and Gary Wallace in the northernmost region of the state, Richmond in the east, and Evansville Reitz in the south. Gerstmeyer even spread it out among two other states, losing to a team from Lexington, Kentucky, while handily beating a squad from Chrisman, Illinois. The Black Cats had one scare in the sectional, a 44–42 victory over bitter rival Terre Haute Garfield. The regional was no problem: an eighteen-point rout of Brazil, a nine-point win against Martinsville. The semistate was a lot tougher—49–46 over Jeffersonville, 55–44 over Evansville Central.

Elkhart, which finished the season second in the polls, brought a 25–3 record into its first trip to the finals. The Blue Blazers won their first five games before stumbling, 59–53, against Muncie Central. They won five more games, lost to Michigan City and fell to Fort Wayne North, then ended the regular season with six consecutive victories.

Elkhart opened the sectional with a convincing ten-point win over Middlebury but barely edged Nappanee, 48–47. The remaining two sectional games and the regional posed few problems—the closest game was a nine-point victory against defending state champion South Bend Central in the regional final. The semistate was a little tougher, but the Blue Blazers advanced with a 47–43 triumph over Lafayette and a 65–53 win over Hammond.

Muncie Central brought the poorest record but shiniest credentials into the finals: a high ranking, a North Central Conference title, and all that tournament tradition. The Bearcats had the luxury of what many called an easy draw and an easy sectional. McCreary cautioned, "When you think you have an easy draw, that's when you get hit in the back of the head with a rock. There isn't any such thing as an easy draw." His players made it look easy, demolishing Cowan, 89–38, and then routing Daleville, 94–32. City rival Burris hung close in the finals, but Central never trailed and won, 63–54. Central routed Union City in the regional opener, then overcame an early 15–8 deficit and survived a scare with Middletown, 57–52.

The Bearcats endured the toughest Sweet Sixteen draw in the state, defeating previously top-ranked Fort Wayne North, 62–48, in the afternoon and then handing unbeaten Mississinewa (27–0) a 63–48 defeat. Muncie Central's 69.9 scoring average and 25.6-point average winning margin were tops among the Final Four teams.

But the biggest statistics of all—and the ones that often doomed opposing teams before they took the court—were already written in the record books. The Bearcats came into the 1954 state championship with twenty-eight sectional titles, sixteen regional titles, ten semistate titles, and four state championships.

Muncie Central also had a supremely confident coach in Jay McCreary.

"I thought," McCreary says now, "I had the ballclub to win the state."

Milan didn't need to worry much about Muncie Central during the week of the finals, since it drew Gerstmeyer in the second afternoon game. The week began with no school on Monday because of a water shortage, but that didn't dampen preparations for the state tournament. Chris Volz scurried to find the Cadillacs to transport the team to the capital. Principal Cale Hudson made plans to distribute Milan's allotment of 950 tickets. Marvin Wood tried to keep his players focused on Gerstmeyer.

Wood told a reporter early that week, "Gerstmeyer's the team to beat Saturday, so we're not worried about any other team right now. I know Gerstmeyer is strong. I understand the two games they lost they were at their lowest of the season."

Indianapolis *News* sportswriter Angelo Angelopolous wrote from Milan, "No one around here—at least with the ball club—is wasting time talking about the glory little Milan has attained in still being alive in the state high school basketball tournament, even though the casualty list now is: 4 alive, 747 dead."

Says Plump, "We knew a little bit about what to expect, not just from the game standpoint but we knew what to expect in the week before. We also knew we could compete against any school we played. I think in '53 we were surprised that we could compete against some of the teams. That was the biggest thing—our confidence level was higher. In '53, we were experimenting with things we didn't know if we could do or not. The cat-and-mouse was one of those things. We had a year to perfect it. I think other teams were at a disadvantage more than we were, because if we got ahead they knew they were going to have to chase a lot."

More than two hours to the west, Howard Sharpe was trying to prepare his team for the Indians. He contradicted himself with every interview. At one point Sharpe said, "We're five to ten points better than our state runner-up of last year. I've seen a good many of the best teams in the state, and I have at least three boys I wouldn't swap for any other three I've looked at. You can say a word or two and turn this team's scoring on and off like a faucet."

Just when someone began to call Sharpe overconfident, he would switch gears. He said, "The state finals field this year is far stronger than last year. We lost our golden opportunity last year, I'm afraid. I was pleased at the draw until I got the scouting reports from the Indianapolis Semifinals last Sunday morning. I've been sick ever since."

As the two coaches worried about each other, Milan residents battled over tickets. Officials removed more than twenty names from the lottery list because no one could confirm or identify the people. "They were putting dead people on the list," says Wood.

The huge frenzy over tickets for the finals culminated in an attempted theft on Tuesday night at the high school. The Indianapolis *Star* reported, "Thugs who hammered open a safe in the Milan High School office Tuesday night in the hope of finding cash received from the sale of tickets to Saturday's championship game of the Indiana high school basketball tournament went away empty-handed. There was no money in the safe and the would-be thieves ignored teacher payroll checks. . . . The money received for tickets from fans of the Milan Indians had been placed in a bank before the burglary attempt." The thieves took only thirty cents, found on the desk of the secretary for superintendent Willard Green.

One of the major plights facing the Indians became evident through a photograph that week in the Indianapolis *News*. It showed Bob Engel stretched out on a table while assistant coach Marc Combs administered heat lamp and vibrator treatment to help ease the pain in his back. Engel's back had taken a bad turn following his stellar performance in the regional and semistate. The same injury that had caused him to miss a good portion of the regular season had worsened. He would start, but it was doubtful that he could go the distance in both games. That meant either Cutter or Wendelman would have to produce on Saturday in Butler Fieldhouse.

The rest of the Indian team appeared healthy and ready. Plump was coming off his twenty-eight-point effort against Attucks, while Craft had tallied thirteen points in that same game. White and Truitt had been consistent in the semistate. The reserves, especially Cutter and Wendelman, knew they might be needed at any moment.

Wood and his team assembled for the traditional Friday morning pep rally in the school gymnasium before leaving in the Cadillacs for Indianapolis. Freda Whitlach, compiling that book on the town's 100th birthday, spoke again at this pep session. She was nearing the end of the book and needed a fitting conclusion. She told the team that two more victories in Indianapolis would provide a fairy-tale ending. It also would help boost sales.

In Terre Haute, four area high schools gathered to wish Gerstmeyer well in a huge pep session. Raymond "Pete" Jolly, coach of Muncie Central's state champion teams in 1928 and 1931, gave a short speech at the public send-off for the favored Bearcats. Elkhart, because of the long drive to Indianapolis, held an early-morning rally before the trek to the capital.

Milan received much of the attention as the teams rolled into Indianapolis. Bob Collins had written a long article in that morning's Indianapolis *Star* singing the school's praises.

> Their story undoubtedly is one of the most refreshing in the history of state high school basketball. The tale has a definite beginning

but at present no foreseeable future. . . . [In '53] they rammed into South Bend Central and took a very convincing licking. So back they went. And those who like emotion with their basketball wept large tears and sang mournful songs of how bad it was that 10 or 12 years more would pass before another little guy shoved into the state finals. . . . The Indians had captured and retained that one thing that often equalized the big and the small in basketball— confidence. It was always there for the taking, but the one thing other small schools never had been able to harness. . . . Anyway you look at it, win or lose, the Milan story is a happy one. Hoosiers will cherish it, resurrect it and tell it through many more basketball seasons.

Milan arrived in Indianapolis in time for the players to practice and for Wood to attend the annual coaches' banquet. He sat next to Gerstmeyer's Howard Sharpe, and the two began to trade some friendly barbs about Saturday's game. But by the end of the conversation, Wood wasn't laughing.

"He was very superstitious," Wood says. "He didn't even like the Black Cats nickname. He talked a lot about these superstitions. He knew we were going to play a zone defense. He told me that zones were no problem. He said there were thirteen ways to beat a zone. We had only talked about four or five. I thought we were going to really learn something tomorrow."

Wood didn't need to remind anyone about the previous year's conduct when the team checked into the Pennsylvania Hotel for the fourth time in the past two years. "Gene White had given them a pep talk," Wood says. "He talked about all the shenanigans they had pulled the year before. We had a mission. The mission was to win the state."

The team ate dinner at the Apex Grill, took a walk outside the hotel, and then settled in for a quiet evening. There wasn't much left to talk about. A good night's sleep was at the top of the agenda. "I can't even remember what we did," says Plump. "I just know the sirens kept waking me up."

After breakfast, the team took another walk, then returned to the hotel for a final period of relaxation. Police escort Pat Stark arrived around noon. The Indians made it to the Fieldhouse midway through the first quarter of the Muncie Central–Elkhart contest.

"It didn't make much difference to us who won that game,"

says Wood. "Our only hope was that it would be a knock-down, drag-out game from beginning to end. We didn't want them to have much energy left for the night game."

Ron Stork hit a free throw to give Elkhart a 1–0 lead against Muncie Central in the opening game. It was the only lead Elkhart would have. The Bearcats led 12–10 after the first quarter and stretched that to 26–23 at the half, then to 41–36 after three quarters. Muncie Central scored the first three points in the final stanza to lead 44–36, but Elkhart made it interesting. The Blue Blazers trailed by just 50–46 with 1:29 remaining, but the Bearcats converted on a barrage of free throws to win 59–50 and reach the final game for the third time in four years.

The Milan players went to the locker room midway through the third quarter and progressed through their normal pre-game preparations. Wood discussed the Gerstmeyer team one player at a time, and someone said a prayer. Everything else was finished. They had worked exactly one year to get back to Butler Field-house for another chance at the state crown. It was time to play the game.

"We were scared," admits Plump. "We hoped we didn't show it but I think we were. I also think we were having a pretty good time. The atmosphere wasn't any different than any of the other tournament games because Marvin kept things in perspective."

The Indians played a zone and rattled the Black Cats for four quarters. Gerstmeyer star Arley Andrews scored just nine points, and the Black Cats never really threatened.

Milan led 21–12 after the first period, 29–23 at the half, and 39–34 after three quarters. The Indians pulled away for good in the fourth and won, 60–48. Perhaps the biggest story in that game was not the game-high twenty-six points from Plump but the play of Cutter off the Milan bench. It was obvious early in the game that Engel's back wouldn't last, and Cutter played his role with three points and some gutsy work inside.

"There were no real surprises," says Wood. "They did exactly what our scouting reports told us they would do. We tried to use our offense to get as many one-on-one situations as possible. After the game someone said, 'Coach Sharpe is going to have to find another way to beat a zone.'"

For Milan, playing the second afternoon game was a new experience. Both first-round victories in the regional and semistate had been in the opening game. Playing the second game meant not only less rest but also little preparation time for the final against Muncie Central. Maybe it's best that the Indian players didn't have a lot of time to think about Central's storied past. Maybe it's best they just got some rest and then played the game. The team dressed quickly after the win over Gerstmeyer, and Pat Stark led them from Butler Fieldhouse back to the Apex Grill for a quick meal. Wood briefly discussed the scouting report on the Bearcats, and then it was time to head back to the Fieldhouse.

On the return trip, the players began to realize the extent of their accomplishments. The once-secluded Pennsylvania Hotel was overrun with fans when the team piled into the Cadillacs for the short ride. The Indians had lost the first game in '53, and no one had really cared what they did in the afternoon. Now they would play for the championship. They were the people's choice, and the people followed them.

"When we were coming back in the afternoon, people would see us and just stop and applaud," said Schroder. "I wasn't used to that. You were just some kid from who knows where and you hadn't accomplished anything that great. That was probably because I didn't put it in the right perspective. I wasn't royalty. I wasn't the king. That just kind of struck me."

Says White, "The Milan thing, whatever it was, was established by the time we got into the final game."

As much as the Milan "thing" was established, it would not last unless the Indians actually won the tournament. They did have one ironic advantage over the Bearcats—experience. Milan started five seniors, and all had been part of the '53 state finalist team. Muncie Central started three juniors and two sophomores. The Bearcats had the banners, but the Indians had the game experience.

"They were big and strong," says Wood. "Muncie Central had the tradition. We knew they would try to kill us on the boards with their physical strength. We had to keep them from getting the second shot. We knew they would gamble a lot. We knew they would want to run."

Given all of the success in the past two years, Wood wasn't about to change his pre-game ritual. But this time the prayer may have been a little stronger. "No matter how good or how tough you might be, you always need help," says Engel. "I've always believed we have a helper, whether you want to believe it or not. There's got to be something that motivates you."

The Bearcats led early at 3–0, but Milan tied the score at 7 and then led 14–11 at the end of the first quarter. Plump, so great in scoring fifty-four points in the two previous games, struggled, but Craft picked up the slack with six points in the first period. The Bearcats, on the other hand, hit just 19 percent of their field-goal attempts and found themselves in an uphill battle. Engel's back already had him on the bench for the Indians, replaced again by Cutter. Craft and Truitt combined for the first five points of the second quarter to extend Milan's advantage to 19–11. Gene Flowers then tried to bring Muncie Central back into the game. He scored six points in a short stretch, and the Bearcats were within 23–17 at the half.

There were several big stories in the first half. First, Cutter had played well in replacing the injured Engel. Plump was cold with just five points, but Craft had scored eleven. Finally, poor shot selection had cost Muncie Central dearly. The Bearcats followed that 19 percent in the first period with 30 percent in the second quarter. Percentages like that would not win the state championship.

"When I watch the film," says Schroder, "I think, boy, did they ever shoot some crazy shots in the first half. The second half was completely different. There was a marked difference in the way they played in the first half and in the second half."

The Bearcats wasted little time in climbing back into the game early in the third quarter. Bob Crawford hit two free throws and Flowers added a long jumper that cut the Milan advantage to 23–21. The Indians then went into what amounted to a patient, deliberate offense rather than a full-fledged cat-and-mouse. They still led 26–24 when Muncie Central reserve Leon Agullana's field goal tied the game just as the third period ended.

Bearcat forward Jim Hinds broke the tie with two free throws early in the fourth quarter that gave Muncie Central a 28–26 advantage, its first lead since the opening period.

This is where Milan began to make history. Until this point, the game was like any other closely contested state championship. A two-point lead. The final quarter. Most people expected a shootout to the finish. Marvin Wood, whose team had been outscored 11–3 in the second half, saw the game slipping away and called for the cat-and-mouse—the only time he did it when behind.

Wood ordered Plump to dribble the ball near midcourt and simply hold it. More than six minutes remained in the game.

"We decided we were just going to hold the ball if they were going to play back and clog the middle and shut off the back door," says Wood. "They just sucked back in around the basket. If they weren't going to come and get us, we would just hold it. We would count on our experience beating their young kids at the end of the game."

Muncie Central wasn't about to chase Milan—not with a two-point lead in the fourth quarter of the state championship game. But McCreary couldn't believe what he saw from the Bearcat bench: Plump holding the ball, not moving.

"I was wondering what he was going to do with it," McCreary says. "We're two ahead and he's standing out there holding the ball. If we were playing today, we would have put a little more pressure on them. In those days, you made them come to you."

For Plump, this particular cat-and-mouse may have been a blessing in disguise. His performance thus far had not been noteworthy. He was having what he would later call his "worst game of the tournament."

"I was thankful to stand out on center court and not do anything," says Plump. "I don't remember thinking very much except that I didn't want to make a mistake. I didn't want to lose the ball. I knew if we could stay within two points that we had a chance. I think it's one of the most unusual things I have ever seen. I meet people all the time who say, 'I saw that game and I went to get a beer, and you were still standing there when I came back.'"

The remaining four Milan players did exercises in the left corner of the floor. "During the stall, I really didn't know what to do," says Cutter. "I was trying to keep my head in the game, trying to be ready for whatever happened. I just tried to stay out of the way."

Wendelman replaced Cutter for quickness with three minutes remaining, and Milan went into its regular offense. Plump missed an outside shot. Muncie Central grabbed the rebound, but a bad pass gave the ball back to the Indians. Craft tied the score on a field goal with just 2:12 left to play. Milan got the ball back

93

again, and Jimmy Barnes fouled Plump, who connected on the two free throws for a 30–28 Indian lead. The clock showed just 1:42 left.

Another Muncie Central turnover, its fourth in the quarter, gave Milan a chance to seal the victory. And it looked like the Indians would when Craft broke loose for a layup, but the ball rolled out to give the Bearcats new life. Flowers hit a driving one-hander to tie the game at 30 with forty-eight seconds left. Plump held the ball until just eighteen seconds remained and called time.

"We decided Plump was going to shoot," said Wood. "He was bigger than the player defending him, Jimmy Barnes. The big problem was what to do with the other players. Then White says, 'Why don't we just move all of the players away from the center?' "

The plan, by now, is legendary. Craft was to inbound the ball to Plump, who would let the clock tick down and then take Barnes one-on-one. It seemed simple enough until Plump took the ball out of bounds. McCreary thought he knew the plan until Plump took the ball out.

"We had to shuffle around when he took the ball out," McCreary says. "We wanted to force him right. They had forced everybody to the left side of the court. I tried to tell Jim not to go for his fake."

Says Plump, "I didn't think that if I missed the shot that the world would end. I really never thought about missing the shot. I never thought about the consequences of hitting it. It was a one-on-one situation, and I had done it I don't how many times."

Plump waited until the clock hit five, then made his move. He made the fake that McCreary knew was coming, and Barnes went for it. Plump then dribbled, pulled up, and hit the shot. Muncie Central was so shocked that the thought of a time-out didn't cross anybody's mind.

"Jim made one mistake in the entire ballgame," says McCreary. "He went for the fake. The ball just fell through and time ran out. Nobody called time-out like that back then. That was the ballgame."

Said McCreary after the game back in '54, "You have to figure that every good ballplayer is at least a .300 shooter. There were seven chances against three that Plump's shot, when he took it, would miss. We couldn't keep him from shooting without risking a foul. We had to let him shoot but planned to make him shoot off-balance or from a difficult angle. We did all we could, but he went up and shot it, and the ball went in and we lost a ball-game."

Very few of the Milan players remember what happened after Plump hit the shot that seemed to stop time temporarily.

Says Plump, "It was kind of euphoria and a relief. Absolute pandemonium broke out. After that, it all became a blur."

Says Wood, "There was just a deafening roar. I cannot remember a gym ever being louder. I remember looking at my old high school coach sitting there. He had been a great coach. He had won sectionals, but he had never even won a regional. Some guys dedicate their entire lives and never make it to a Final Four. I thought, here I am only twenty-six years old and winning the state championship."

The scene quieted long enough for the players to receive their championship rings. Then it was time for the Trester Award, the honor given for mental attitude. A player from the championship team had never received the Trester Award. Someone from the crowd yelled, "Go ahead and give it to Plump." Plump did win the award. A few weeks later, he became the first person in the history of Indiana high school basketball to win the state championship, the Trester Award, and Mr. Basketball.

In the Muncie Central locker room, McCreary spoke to his somber troops. "Boys," he said, "I'm really proud of you. You gave all you had and I'll never ask for any more. If we had to do it over again, we'd do it the same way."

Virtually every media outlet in Indiana gathers for the state tournament, and it took the Milan players a long time before they could return in peace to the locker room. They said a short prayer and then reminded Pat Stark of his promise.

"Our dressing room was a pretty quiet place," says Wood. "We were happy, but we didn't show much more emotion than after we had won the regional or the semistate. We were just savoring the moment."

Says Schroder, "I don't know how you would describe it. Everybody was just overwhelmed. Nobody had ever thought what would happen if we really did win it. Everybody played it one game at a time, and then all of a sudden there it was."

In retrospect, the post-game celebration may seem relatively mild. Stark led the team from Butler Fieldhouse and took them on their zany wrong-way trip three times around Monument Circle. The motorcade then returned to the Pennsylvania Hotel, where the team would spend the night before departing for home on Sunday morning. There just weren't too many other places teenage boys could celebrate winning the state championship after midnight. Given their simple nature, they were probably happiest just going back to the hotel.

"We celebrated the state by drinking Cokes and watching TV," says White.

Says Cutter, "We had pillow fights, water fights, just good old fun. We didn't go anyplace else. We just had fun as a group. It was the first night I ever remember where I stayed up all night. Other times, you were thinking about games, going over what the coach said you needed to do. This time we didn't have anything to look forward to. We had just done it."

One thing was definitely certain. No matter how much fun the team had that night, no matter how it celebrated, no one could have ever predicted what would happen the next afternoon on the return trip to Milan.

That's when lives really began to change.

7 *The Aftermath*

After they had celebrated Saturday night, the Milan players thought reality would come quickly in the morning. They were wrong.

In retrospect, winning the championship may have been the easy part. Dealing with the aftermath became difficult. The team, accustomed to playing big games in front of capacity crowds, wasn't familiar with giving speeches to a crowd estimated at more than twenty times the population of the town.

The day started when Marvin Wood took the troops for breakfast at the Apex Grill. This time, the meal was on the house. After breakfast, the team went to mass at a Catholic church near the hotel ("I don't even know if any of us were Catholics," says Roger Schroder), and then prepared for the trip home.

They began to get a partial understanding of what they had accomplished by reading the morning papers. The media had billed this game as David versus Goliath in the days leading to the tournament. David had won, had actually beaten a team that had already captured four state titles. At a time when many people

97

discussed the possibility of class basketball, tiny Milan had done the impossible.

The players had viewed it as just another game. The people viewed it as the game of the century.

Bob Collins, who would become an honorary mayor of Milan later that day, wrote Sunday morning:

> And the game—well it was one of the greatest this state tourney has ever seen and the Butler Fieldhouse was a madhouse as the final gun sounded last night. What a night for Milan. Not only did this school, with an enrollment of 162 (73 boys), become the smallest school to win this title since Thorntown licked the field in 1915, it now is the only school ever to win and still get a mental attitude award recipient. The Trester medal kid was, of course, Plump—the mightiest Redskin of all. The award gave Robert a grip on just about everything but the fieldhouse doorknobs. He also was the best scorer in the semifinals and finals with 81 points—the last two of which will not be forgotten in Indiana for years.

Most players looked forward to the two-hour return trip to Milan as a chance to catch up on some sleep or to relive the game. There was time for neither.

No interstate linked Indianapolis and Cincinnati in those days, so the Cadillacs, paced by patrolman Pat Stark, went home on the back roads. The team drove through Shelbyville and took a couple of victory laps around the town square, where about a thousand people paid homage to the champions. In Greensburg, someone had pulled a cattle truck onto the square and painted a sign on the side that read, "Congratulations Milan."

As the caravan continued down old State Road 46, the team began to realize that the reception in Milan would be big, much bigger than anyone had expected. The Cadillacs turned onto State Road 101 headed for Penntown, where cars and people lined both sides of the road. There were still eleven miles to Milan. "It was steady traffic from that point in," says Rollin Cutter.

"I remember as we were traveling into town, there were so many people that weren't even on the sidewalks," says Wood. "They were in the streets. It was hard to imagine it was taking place."

Says Schroder, "A traffic jam to us was like six cars, not that many miles."

The caravan stopped just outside the city limits, and two seniors—Ray Craft and Ken Wendelman—climbed onto the hood of the lead Cadillac. They put the state championship trophy between them and rode into town, much like conquerors returning from routing a foe in battle.

There were people everywhere, on the sidewalks, in the streets, hanging from trees, standing on vehicles. The men wore their Sunday best (after all, it was Sunday), and the women wore dresses. It was the peak of a decade, of a lifetime.

Look unknowingly at the pictures and it might appear to be a riot. Or one of those gatherings where thousands welcomed home the heroes of World War II. But this was a high school basketball team, a group of teenagers.

"It really caused a stir in the state," says Gene White. "You could just see nothing but people. That's not true anymore. You might get five or ten thousand people, but nothing like that."

The estimates range from 20,000 to 40,000 people. In the years that have passed, probably 100,000 said they attended the celebration.

The throng assembled near the school, where workers had constructed a makeshift stage on the back of a flatbed truck. Every player and coach took a turn at the microphone. Patrolman Pat Stark cried when his time came. Collins and Robert Terry of the Cincinnati *Post* earned honorary mayor citations.

But tiny Mary Lou Wood, wife of the winning coach, stole the show. Talk to the players today, and every one remembers her words of wisdom.

She says now, "I'll never forget that moment. It was like a sea of people. I remember looking around the bend [of the stage] and seeing those kids. I hadn't thought of one word. I hadn't even thought of being up there. It seemed like a dream."

She took the stage, looked at the crowd, and muttered just one sentence.

"It's nice to be important," she said, "but it's more important to be nice."

The words echoed out to the thousands of people, and the Milan players took them to heart. No player can even remember what he said on that day, but all remember Mary Lou Wood.

The team members ate dinner at the local country club and then went their separate ways. That was the first time the players had been apart for three days. They had accomplished everything possible for a high school team, but they also knew in the backs of their minds that they would never be together as a team again. Some players would return for more seasons, but the nucleus would graduate in May.

"We were seniors, we were going different directions," says Engel. "That was kind of a letdown to think, 'Where are my buddies going to go?' After it all sank in and it all settled down, you get to thinking that this was the last shot."

Wood quickly put an end to that thinking. He announced that the team would not wait twenty-five, or even five, years to hold a reunion. This special team would get together every year, to maintain contact, to keep the dream alive. Wood still coordinates that annual reunion, and many players plan their vacations around it.

The celebration didn't end on Sunday night. The superintendent canceled school on Monday for another rally, and Wood admits that education took a backseat to athletics for the remainder of the year. Town officials on Monday urged celebrants to bring a bucket of water to the bonfire because of the town shortage.

The media also hit with another barrage on Monday. Many of the Indiana papers at the state finals didn't have a Sunday edition, so most of the game accounts appeared on Monday. By this time, everyone who had any interest knew all of the details. This was a chance for the Monday papers to wax philosophical and put this victory in perspective.

The Associated Press sent out a story that read, "Members of the Indiana High School Athletic Association won't have any difficulty remembering the year of their 50th anniversary. Milan's new state basketball champs made it a memorable one by stomping on most of the superstitions that have accumulated in modern Hoosier prep basketball and kicking them under the bleachers of Butler Fieldhouse Saturday night. The good little team beat the good big team, which isn't supposed to be done. The team from the small town licked the city boys, and that hadn't happened since Thorntown won the 1915 tourney."

From Jep Cadou Jr. of the Indianapolis *Star:* "Yes, we picked Muncie Central. We picked them back on St. Valentine's Day and we never regretted the choice for a single moment. They were our team and they are our team. We were immensely proud of the Bearcats in the dark moment of defeat. They never quit. They played courageous basketball. They took their defeat like the big men they are. But the Bearcats had the misfortune to find themselves smack in the path of a team of destiny. As someone who was riding the same bandwagon with this writer exclaimed, 'They had to be perfect to beat Muncie.' They were, those great little men who surely must have put an end for all time to this foolish talk of having a basketball tournament divided into classes.''

From Cy McBride at the Richmond *Palladium:* ''There are so many great things one could write and say about this Milan basketball team that our efforts seem somewhat futile. There aren't enough superlatives to describe appropriately the accomplishments of Coach Marvin Wood's Indians. One statement can be made with finality. We look forward to seeing hundreds of basketball games between now and the time we give up and stay home by our television set. We feel certain none will compare with the game we were fortunate enough to view Saturday night at Butler Fieldhouse.''

There were mixed emotions in Muncie, where the town had planned a welcome parade and a day-long slate of activities long before Central had played its first game at Butler. They couldn't celebrate another state championship, so they celebrated the season. It was, after all, many said, a trip to the finals, and their team did lose with class and dignity. Many thought it was a fluke and treated it as such. Others repeated that old phrase of eternal optimism, ''There's always next year.''

Under a headline ''But There Is No Joy in Mudville,'' Bob Barnet wrote in Monday's edition of the Muncie *Star,* ''In the meantime, kind friends, don't waste any sympathy on us Muncie folks. We'll get over that two-point near miss. We'll get well— we'll live. We'll get over it in a hurry. All we need is three or four months.''

Herb Silverburg of the Muncie *Evening Press* wrote in a column titled ''Monday-After Hangover'': ''It will be questionable about how many of the several thousand Muncie fans down at Indianapolis ever voted for Adlai Stevenson. But one and all, they would have agreed with the Democratic chieftain that November night in 1952 when he commented for the television, 'It hurts too much to laugh and I'm too old to cry.' That's the way Muncie felt Saturday evening for it was tough to take and a lot of us will be weeks getting over the effects.''

For the next three months, people from all over the country visited Milan. They wanted a tour of the town and the high school. They wanted to catch a glimpse of Wood and Plump. The stories weren't good enough. They had to see for themselves.

"It was like we were on exhibit," says Wood. "There was some school, but it was limited."

School secretary Betty Dobson sorted mail and telegrams from all over the country. The most famous was the one addressed to "Bobby Plump, Plump, Indiana." The letter made it to Plump, and he cherishes it as his favorite.

Immediately after the victory, Wood was on everybody's list of after-dinner speakers. He was down-to-earth, funny, and a good model for other coaches and players. In all, he made eighty-six public appearances in the months following the tournament. Other schools also called. Some wanted Wood to fill an existing vacancy. Others said they would create a position if Wood would coach their team.

He knew he was happy in Milan, but he also knew that he couldn't accomplish anything more there. He was just twenty-six years old, and everything else would be downhill. He eventually took the job at New Castle, a much bigger school that played in the prestigious North Central Conference.

The thought of coaching at New Castle thrilled Wood. If he could have as much success as he had at Milan, think what would happen at the bigger New Castle. He stayed at New Castle just two years, coached several other schools, and never had the success that he had at tiny Milan.

Seven of the ten players on that '54 team graduated just a few months after the state finals. Bob Plump, Ray Craft, and Ken Wendelman enrolled at Butler, Gene White and Roger Schroder at Franklin, and Ron Truitt at Houston. Bob Engel chose to bypass college, despite the fact that several teams offered him scholarships.

Some familiar faces remained when Milan opened the 1954–55 regular season. Glenn Butte, Rollin Cutter, and Bill Jordan returned, as did '54 alternates Bob Wichman and Kenny Delap. It just wasn't the same. Wood was gone, replaced by Jim Rousch. The team was good, winning the sectional the next two years, but it could never get over that regional hump that had frustrated Milan for most of its existence.

It would be nineteen years until Milan finally won another regional title in 1973. The team lost in the semistate amid a million comparisons to the '54 champions.

But life was different in the seventies. People had other things to do besides concentrating on basketball for twenty-four hours a day. The magic wasn't there. This team, no matter that it reached the Sweet Sixteen, was destined to be a footnote in Milan history. "We had an exciting time in '73, but nobody remembers that," says Dobson.

No one wanted to remember that team because no one wanted to forget the '54 squad.

The Indians finally hit bottom in the 1990–91 season, losing every game they played. No one's really to blame, except maybe the system. Basketball in Milan is just not a life-and-death proposition anymore. There are too many other variables.

Every one of the ten players on that '54 team went on to success in his own way, whether it be in public or private life. Eight of those ten players graduated from college, something totally unplanned before the Indians won the championship. One even made it to Hollywood.

Milan became the model for other small schools. It still is today. It became the story for a major motion picture. No one has matched it, and no one likely ever will.

Probably most people in '54 thought that another school would duplicate Milan's feat, if not next season then in the next decade. After all, hadn't Thorntown done virtually the same thing in 1915? Yes, and no. Thorntown had played in a tourney with just 155 teams, while Milan had played in one with 751 squads. Thorntown had defeated Montmorenci in the championship game. Milan beat Muncie Central.

"After all these years," says Gene White, "it's looking like a bigger feat than we thought."

8 *Coach Marvin Wood*

It's unusually warm for a Sunday afternoon in February, but basketball is in season. Marvin Wood, thirty some years and 284 miles from Milan, is still on the bench, but he is watching the clock run down on his basketball career. He is in his ninth season as the head coach at Saint Mary's College, a small Indiana school of about 2,000 women directly across Highway 33 from Notre Dame.

Wood's team has struggled while playing its first season in Division III after a lifetime in the NAIA. The Belles are 9–7, but today's contest against Rosary, a small women's college outside of Chicago which has the ninth-ranked NAIA team in the country, does not look promising. "I just hope we don't get embarrassed," Wood says as he watches his team go through warmups. The Belles had dropped a decision to Hope College the day before, a game that Wood said might have lifted them into the postseason tournament as an independent had they won.

On this Sunday afternoon at Angela Athletic Facility on the Saint Mary's campus, Wood looks far removed from the high school game on which he left an indelible mark in 1954. The gym is built into the ground and holds about 1,000 people, but only one side of the bleachers is utilized for games. Saint Mary's has no band, no cheerleaders, no halftime show. The concession stand is one table filled with two-liter bottles of soft drinks and candy bars, and the lone worker keeps the money in an aged pencil box. This is definitely not big-time basketball.

"I don't know too much about them," Wood says honestly of his opponent. "I just know that they're probably pretty good."

That's another benefit of this job—little, if any, scouting. This is one of the few schools where the main athletic emphasis remains on fun. Wood still looks in his element on the bench. He jokes with the officials, talks with the opposing coach, acts as if he doesn't have a care in the world. He doesn't look like the man who made history so long ago, and he definitely doesn't look like a man who was diagnosed as having lymphatic cancer just a few years ago.

"I feel a lot less pressure at Saint Mary's," Wood says. "The pressure I have at Saint Mary's is self-imposed. We want to have success. We want to represent the school well. We want to have a solid program. We want the girls to have fun. We want to have class."

Just minutes before the game is set to begin, Wood takes the team aside in the first few rows of the bleachers and delivers his pre-game talk. One of the keys will be to keep the much bigger and more physical Rosary squad outside. The crowd will play no role in this game; there is no homecourt advantage. Fewer than a hundred fans sit in the bleachers at tipoff, and that includes a handful of students riding stationary bicycles that overlook the court.

Saint Mary's scores the first five points of the game, but Rosary storms back to tie the game at 12 and then scores nine of the next eleven points for a 21–14 advantage. The Belles stay within striking distance the rest of the half and trail 47–37 at the intermission.

They're not getting embarrassed like Wood had feared, but they still have a long way to go in the second half. It will be nothing new for Wood. He already has come a long way.

Wood takes his team into the locker room for the halftime talk. The locker room at Saint Mary's College is about the size of the closets at the university across the highway. There are lockers on opposite sides of the room, a large chalkboard, two small benches, and a door. The room is so cramped that there's not room for all of the players to sit on the two benches. "Not a bad job, girls," he says as they enter the room trailing by ten points.

He conducts the same halftime ritual that he started way back at French Lick in the early fifties. He writes "DEFENSE" in large letters on one side of the board. Under that, he writes, "1. Get back, 2. Shooters, 3. Pick-up ball, 4. Boards." He puts "OFFENSE" in those same big letters on the other side of the board. Under that he writes, "1. Pick up man-to-man, 2. Run, 3. vs. zone 2–3, rotate."

His halftime message is short and to the point. He emphasizes the phrases on the board and then delivers a few parting words. "Shut off the break and pick up quick on defense," he says. "We have to cut down on our errors. They're a good team but we can play with them."

It looks like that embarrassment might come early in the second half. Rosary goes ahead 57–39 and still leads 65–48 with just over eleven minutes left in the game. But the Belles score nine unanswered points to pull within 65–57. Rosary finally calls a time-out with 8:28 left and the lead cut to 68–63.

Saint Mary's forces another Rosary time-out with 3:42 left when a short jumper cuts the margin to 77–74. That is the closest the Belles will get. Rosary wins, 83–76.

• • •

Marvin Wood was just twenty-four years old when he interviewed for the Milan coaching position in 1952. He was young, energetic, soft-spoken, and made in the mold of his Butler University coach, Tony Hinkle, an Indiana legend whose own roots were to Amos Alonzo Stagg. Wood had played three years for Hinkle at Butler, then spent the next two years as head coach at French Lick—where, four years later, Larry Bird was born.

For a variety of reasons, the Milan job was enticing to Marvin and Mary Lou Wood. First, it was a step up in terms of competition and visibility. It was also closer to their hometowns. Finally, the team he was to coach had a lot of young talent returning from what had been a decent 1952 season. "Young coaches always have to look for talent," Wood says. "That's the way you win and that's the way you build your recognition."

"If you say 'Marvin Wood,' I see a nice big round face with not much hair on his head, with a nice big smile and a pleasant voice," says longtime school secretary Betty Dobson. "He and his wife carried a jolly personality. You immediately felt like you knew them. They were very warm and responsive. You couldn't help but like them. He exuded warmth. By the way he lived, he gave an example to you. He didn't have to say he didn't drink or he didn't smoke. You could just see it."

The players found a likable coach and an instant friend in Wood. He rarely raised his voice, but everyone knew he meant business when he did speak. Bob Engel remembers just one time when Wood lost his temper. "A student manager came down and told us what we were going to work on because he had to attend a teachers' meeting. You know how guys will do. Everybody was kind of playing around. We were shooting set shots half-court. All of a sudden, the door slammed. Mr. Wood walked out there and blew his whistle. He said, 'I'm observing things here. You boys seem to be having fun. I don't think this was on the practice agenda. I want you guys to remember one thing: You play like you practice.' When we went home that night, my tongue was hanging in my shoelaces. That was the only time I can remember that the man raised his voice or got upset."

The young coach took a simple approach to the game. He had his offensive and defensive patterns. He had his game plan. What he said, he expected the players to follow. But most of all, he wanted his team to have fun.

"I've always viewed basketball as a game," Wood says. "I know a lot of fans don't see it that way. I didn't want to put unnecessary pressure on the boys or myself. I always attempt to be at practice early. I like to run a solid ship. If I say we're going to start practice at four, then we start at four. I rarely had a practice session last more than two hours. After practice, I was the last one to leave."

Wood also knew the Milan job would not be easy, even with the talent. He had to win over a team and a community that had vocally disagreed with the dismissal of former coach Snort Grinstead. He had to convince people the Hinkle system would work on the high school level at Milan. Most of all, he had to win.

He did win—twenty-five victories and just four defeats that first season, including an undreamed-of trip to the state finals. But there was a drawback to that unexpected success: Bigger expectations came the following season, with the team virtually intact.

Wood worked at the huge Seagrams warehouse during the summer of '53. There were no summer basketball camps, and the coach had little if any contact with his players. He gathered the team together on October 1 and began the now-historic march to the state championship.

Wood suddenly became the most marketable coach in the state. The theory was that if he could win the state at Milan, then think what he could do at a bigger school. Name a school and it probably contacted him. Anderson, Monticello, Elkhart—the list goes on and on. Several schools said they would fire their basketball coach if Wood agreed to take the job. Those had no chance with him. He finally settled on New Castle.

When Wood announced his decision, his fan mail turned to hate mail. People accused him of taking a team molded by Grinstead, leading it to the state finals, and then skipping town on the first bus out. "When I first heard it, I thought he was crazy," Plump says. Wood says money had nothing to do with the decision to leave Milan. It was simply time to move on. He had taken the Milan team as far as it could ever go. Everything else would have been anticlimactic.

"It was really difficult to leave for a number of reasons," Wood says. "We had grown attached to the community, and probably more attached to it because of the success we had. We had a number of good players coming back. The program was solid down through the seventh grade. I was talking to [auto dealer] Chris Volz one day and he said, 'You'll never leave the town for money because we'll pay you more than any other school. The school board will pay you for the job there, and you can sell cars for me. You can sell my cars anywhere in the United States.' We didn't leave for money. There was something that was appealing to me about going to a larger school. There were people in the community that were broken-hearted. There were people in the community that were angry."

Things at New Castle didn't turn out quite as Wood expected when he inherited a proud program down on its luck. The

108

Trojans had been 5–17 and had lost to Straughn in the second round of the sectional while Wood was leading Milan to the state title. Their fortunes didn't improve much the next two seasons under Wood. New Castle was 14–11 in 1955 with a sectional championship, then 6–16 in 1956.

Wood found extraordinary pressure at New Castle. Most of that pressure he put on himself.

"I thought that if I had done well at a small school, then I ought to be able to do something similar at a bigger school," Wood said. "It doesn't always work that way, and I found it out. This was self-imposed pressure, wanting to do better than I was actually doing. Everyone wants to be on the top of the ladder, everyone wants to be a winner. The way you measure the best in coaching is by W's. We weren't getting the W's after winning the state the previous year."

His wife noticed the same Wood on the outside, but she could also see that the internal pressure to win was great. He had back problems that "I have no doubt in my mind stemmed from nerves," she says. "I think he put a lot of pressure on himself at New Castle. He never, ever had been one to take medicine. He got to where he was taking aspirin every night before he went to bed. I think he just wanted to do well so badly at a bigger school."

What further compounded those records and the pressure was the promise Wood said he received that construction would begin on a new gymnasium. "We were there the second year and they hadn't turned a stone yet," Wood says. "Three years after I resigned, they started the project. This was something they had promised they would do much earlier." When the gym was completed in 1959, it was—and still is—the largest high school fieldhouse in the world, with a seating capacity of 9,325.

So, Wood resigned at New Castle after just two seasons to take a much bigger challenge as the head coach at North Central, a brand-new high school on the north side of Indianapolis. He started from scratch and found the climb not only uphill, but almost impossible. "It was a lot more difficult than I ever imagined," he says. "There were times the first year or year and a half that I wished I had stayed at New Castle. It was a major-league schedule with a minor-league team."

Wood was determined to build a winner at North Central, and

he spent nine seasons trying. He made it to the finals of the Marion County tourney in four of those nine years and played all of the powerhouses in central Indiana, but the team could not get past the mediocre stage. It struggled more than it succeeded. Complicating matters further was the fact that North Central had three middle schools feeding into it, and each of those three basketball coaches ran a different program.

"We could always be competitive," Wood says, "but being close doesn't satisfy coaches. You want to be at the top of the heap. You want to be a winner and compete for the sectional championship. The superintendent told me that as long as he was there, the program would stay the way it was. I thought that if I wanted to stay in coaching that I had better get out and start looking for communities that wanted to build."

He found such a program in Mishawaka, almost as far north as one can get in Indiana. Things didn't work out again. Wood's mother-in-law suffered a heart attack in that first season, and he thought it would be better if they were closer to her in central Indiana.

Wood resigned after just one season and took the athletic director's position at Shelbyville, the first time in sixteen years that he was not a high school head coach. He also served as the ticket manager for the Golden Bears. "I had more hassles over tickets in three years than I had complaints about coaching in thirty years," Wood says. He became restless at Shelbyville and yearned for another spot on the bench. "It was a new challenge for him and he worked hard at it, but he was not happy," Mary Lou says.

In a bizarre twist of events, the position opened again at Mishawaka, and Wood found himself back as the head coach. The headline in the Shelbyville paper the next day read, "Wood leaves for first love." Says Mary Lou, "I always said if you put a basketball and me in the middle of the floor, I know which one he would choose."

Wood stayed at Mishawaka this time and put together one of the most powerful programs in the state. Perhaps the biggest problem was that—just as professional teams in New York and Los Angeles receive increased publicity by being in media centers—media exposure for Indiana high school basketball is greatest in and close to Indianapolis. Few took notice of those dominant Mishawaka teams. Wood coached eleven teams at

Mishawaka; the Cavemen went 20–3 in 1975, 21–4 in 1976, and they earned Top Ten ratings several of those years. But he couldn't generate the same tournament success as when he had coached at Milan. His teams won just one title while competing in the tough South Bend Sectional. "Our sectional was almost like the state tournament," he says. "If Mishawaka had been anywhere else but there, I think we could have gone to the state a couple of times."

It was time to move again, but this time he made a more dramatic announcement. Wood retired from coaching and moved into a counselor's position at Mishawaka. "I was fifty years old and I thought maybe it was time," he says. "It hadn't been as much fun as it had been. The pressure was just as great as it had been in some of my earlier years. After you're successful, you want to be successful all of the time."

Wood's retirement from coaching lasted less than one year. Mishawaka girls' coach John Taylor suffered a heart attack early in the season, and administrators asked Wood if he would take the team. He hesitated at first because he had never coached girls and wasn't sure if he could make a smooth transition. After that initial doubt, Wood took charge and led the girls to a 22–2 record that included an appearance in the Sweet Sixteen. That was farther than any of his boys' teams at Mishawaka had advanced.

Wood coached a similar group of girls that summer in AAU competition, but Taylor recovered before the start of the next high school season, and Wood was out of coaching again. This time, he approached Saint Mary's with his impressive credentials and said that if the basketball position ever opened, he would be interested. That call came in 1982.

"Their coach walked out on them two weeks before the season started," he recalls. "They had a dispute out there in the athletic department. They said they would rather have a woman coach, but a couple of days later they called and asked me if I would take the job, and I accepted."

Some people thought he was crazy when he first took that position at Saint Mary's, including his wife. "I just couldn't understand why he even wanted to do it," she says. "But I thought he could probably help them." She felt those same feelings at her husband's first game. "No students came to the games, except for maybe the girls' roommates," she says. "I really didn't know

111

what to expect. It was really dead. I had to learn not to yell so much because there was nobody else around."

Wood also admits to some frustration that first year. "The first year was the toughest," he says. He has turned the program around and lifted it a division along the way. He is sometimes at a disadvantage because other schools, unlike Saint Mary's, offer athletic scholarships. But that doesn't worry Wood. He has faced tougher odds than this.

"Coaching to me has always been something exciting," he says. "It's like recess to a small boy. This is like my winter recreation. A lot of coaches say they wish they could get into something like this where they could keep the blood circulating and keep in contact with the sport. That's the most positive place I've worked in my life. There are no scholarships. We just follow up on people who contact Saint Mary's. If a Division I school or a Division II school is interested, I'm out in left field.

"Boys are stronger, bigger, and generally a little quicker. Girls are, generally speaking, more interested in growth development. They will work just as hard or harder at developing their skills. Girls are more patient. Boys all want to be part of the action. Girls want to be part of the team. You don't have the fan support, you don't have the cheerleaders at Saint Mary's. In some ways, that's good. It makes coaching more like a checkers game. It's you and your team against the other coach and his team.

"Some of the things that are inviting to me at this age at Saint Mary's are that our girls go home at Thanksgiving. I get to be with my family. We have a three-week break at Christmas. I get to be with my family, and they get to be with their families. But I'm also nearing the end of the line. It's a little more difficult for me now. I'm afraid that the word A-G-E is creeping in."

• • •

Age is something that Wood has battled all of his life. The fact that he was the youngest coach ever to win a state title—a mark later bested by Muncie Central's Dwight Tallman—put enormous pressure on him to win more championships at bigger schools. The struggles at New Castle, the disagreements over the direction of the program at North Central, the hiatus at Shelbyville, being good but not good enough at Mishawaka—they all weighed heavily on Wood.

"That was a thing that bothered me all the time," he says. "I made a statement that if it had happened later in my life, I probably would have gotten out of coaching at that point. You reach the top and you can't go any higher than that in Indiana high school basketball. Then someone once told me, 'Don't look at it that way. Look at it as a peak you can build on for the rest of your life. It's going to open doors for you that would never have opened.' That's the way it has turned out. A lot of beautiful things have happened in our life because we were part of that unusual championship in Indiana.

"It's been unusual. People remember it. It was in the media for at least thirty years after we won it. Then the movie *Hoosiers* brought it to a new generation. It was a highlight, but how many highlights do you have in your life? And when are they going to happen? When is the best time for them to happen? As I look back, I think it was best for them to happen when you're young because you have all the years to look back and reflect on them. And I think if you live a good life and play your cards right, you can use them in a positive sense the rest of your life. I think a lot of things in my life have been influenced by that. I've gotten my foot in doors I probably couldn't have gotten into had that not happened. You're kind of an example. If you're going to be an example, be a good example."

Wood has always been a good example, a role model for any young coach, or any young person. "Christian living has always been a very important part of my life," he says. "I had great faith from an early age."

His faith helped him through the tragedy of losing his son, Douglas, who was killed in a motorcycle accident in 1979. That came after years of the young man's battles against drugs and alcohol, times that Wood says he lived through because of his great faith.

Wood is fighting his toughest battle now. He was in the midst of an unsuccessful race for state representative when doctors discovered cancer. It eventually forced him to miss the 1991–92 Saint Mary's season because of a lengthy hospital stay in Indianapolis.

"When they told me I had cancer, it was quite a shock," he says. "You hear about other people having it, but I never thought about having it myself. When they told me it was in an advanced stage, it was scary. When you have a disorder like this, you have a lot of down days. I came across some very beautiful people. I had over 300 letters from people, lots of calls from the Milan group.''

The support from the Milan community and his former state championship players shows how much they still mean to each other. Wood still wears his championship ring and has removed it only when competing in sporting events. He organizes every reunion. He, more than anybody else, wants the group to remain together.

''It changed my life, and it changed the lives of the players,'' he says. ''I've seen basketball do so much for so many people. There may be a negative side, but I'm looking at the positive side. We learned some lessons down there that have been very valuable to us as the years have gone by. I love it. That was the very high point in my life. It changed my life for all the years after that.''

9

Bob Plump

Bob Plump's insurance and financial-planning office is a shrine to a lifetime of basketball achievement—plaques, trophies, pictures, letters. He keeps a three-foot stack of letters and packages near a bookshelf, items that have arrived in just the past five years since the release of *Hoosiers*.

His favorite letter, actually a poem, hangs on the wall behind glass in an Indiana-shaped wood plaque. He received it in the second week of June 1987, shortly after *Hoosiers* put Plump back in the national spotlight. The writer was nine-year-old Kyle Wright of Greensfork, who tried to imagine Plump's thoughts during the final ten seconds of the championship game with Muncie Central.

The Shot of Bobby Plump

10. . . . Oh boy!
I am not filled with joy,
With this team's fate behind me,
The shot I take had better be.

9. . . . What am I doing dribbling this ball?
If I fail, we'll probably fall.
If we lose
Our fans will give us boos.

8. . . . Why is this guy guarding me?
To get a win for thee?
I got to start moving soon
Or the game will end at the next full moon.

7. . . . It's a 30 tie!
Well Bearcat, I'll have to say goodbye.
I'm going to dribble now.
I could win it for us. Wow!

6. . . . There, I just got past my man.
Our fans are giving me a great big hand.
I can win this game, I can do it yet.
I'll hit the shot, I'll do it I bet.

5. . . . What am I doing?
The fans are booing.
Now I see.
But it can't be.

4. . . . What happened was, I picked up the ball.
Now the bunch of players are like a wall.
I feel my arms rearing up.
I feel like I'm going to jump.

3. . . . There, I just got rid of the ball.
The thing had better start to fall.

2. . . . The ball just went through the net.
Now we're going to win, I bet.

1. . . . They just took their desperation shot.
But, apparently, they're not too hot.
The shot of theirs, just didn't go,
Because we were a bit too slow.

0. . . . WE WON!

The accompanying letter called Plump "a hero of many young basketball hopefuls." This was thirty-three years after he hit the last-second shot to give Milan the state title. And it was not an unusual occurrence. Plump has received more mail for that one long-ago shot than anyone could imagine. People mention it everywhere—the bank, the office, the restaurants, the games. A recent package contained two tapes of *Hoosiers,* asking for an autograph from the "greatest Hoosier of them all." He averages ten speaking engagements a year solely because he hit that one jump shot.

Through it all, amazingly enough, Plump remains "one of the boys." He has never met a stranger and still possesses an "Aw shucks" attitude. Try to find someone who has a bad thing to say about Bobby Plump. It might take a couple of lifetimes.

He is the first to be surprised at everything that has happened over the past forty years. He once admitted that he often went back to an empty Butler Fieldhouse and just thought about that game, just stared at the dark floor and wondered if it really did happen.

"There are things that happened that I never even thought of, let alone dreamed of," Plump says. "From an athletic standpoint, it would be extremely difficult for anything to compare to the thrills the state tourney provided. There are other things that occurred later in my life that were as significant or more significant, but not for an instantaneous thrill or for long-term gratification."

Plump is the man associated with the miracle. He is the one people seek when they want to talk Milan basketball. Says former teammate Rollin Cutter, "He has continued the legend for so long by his personality. We don't need a publicity agent. We've got Bob. He will talk to you at the drop of a hat. Everybody knows Bob. He's just that kind of guy."

What that state championship did was transform Plump into a different person. He was still the down-home boy, but he could no longer hide in the shadows of small-town obscurity. He was a state hero, and people expected him to act like one. That meant personal appearances and speeches.

"I've become more comfortable with it now," he says. "I was backward and introverted. It was difficult to just stand up and talk before our class. When I was on the basketball floor, all that didn't matter. I knew I could handle myself on the court, but I was never really sure about myself. It was difficult to enjoy at first because it was kind of a painful experience to be out in the public and not know what the public was or what to expect. That didn't mean I didn't enjoy it, but I enjoy it more now.''

• • •

Plump never really knew his mother. She died at home from hemorrhage of the uterus when he was just five. That left his father, Lester, and his sister, Dorothy, to raise him in tiny Pierceville.

"I remember three or four things about my mother," he recalls. "I remember sitting on her lap listening to the radio. When the rest of the kids went to school, I remember standing on a stool drying the dishes. I remember the day she died because my dad kind of stumbled down the stairs and there was a lot of emotion. And I remember they made me kiss her in the casket, which was a big thing back then.''

Plump lived probably the simplest life of any player on that '54 Milan team. His family lived in a two-story house on a dead-end street in Pierceville. They had no electricity until 1948. They had no telephone, definitely no television. His father worked a variety of jobs, including truck driving and factory work. There were six Plump children in all, Bobby the youngest.

In the beginning, of course, Plump was closest to those other three players in Pierceville—Butte, White, and Schroder. His father, like virtually every other father in Indiana in the fifties, built a backboard and goal at the side of the house. Plump and Butte turned on the radio and played along with the state finals in distant Indianapolis. He remembers the '49 tourney in particular, when he was Madison and Butte was Jasper. For the record, Jasper, 9–11 when the tournament began, won that game, 62–61—maybe the biggest upset in tournament history, until Milan. Madison was the team with the glamour player: Dee Monroe, who set a scoring record and was "Mr. Basketball." "We played along with the tournament," Plump says, "but to say that was a goal and a dream, no. It would make a nice story, but that's not true." Boys in Fort Wayne and Kokomo, Evansville and Muncie, boys all over Indiana had done the same thing.

Probably the biggest influence on Plump in those early years was his father. He saw his father get up for work every morning, turn in a full day, and then come home to take care of the family.

118

He learned dedication and discipline through him, something that would help him all of his life. His father died of a stroke in 1966 at the age of sixty-seven, and Bob's two brothers died at fifty-four (heart attack) and fifty-seven (cancer).

Plump talks often about his dad—how he attended every game and kept individual points on a small index card; how he rarely brought the game home to Pierceville from the Milan gym. While everyone in town talked about basketball, the Plump household usually refrained from it.

"Dad was a very religious man," Plump says. "I never heard him raise his voice. I never had an occasion where he laid a hand on any of us. I never heard Dad say anything out of the ordinary, but everyone knew when he did say something that he meant it. He would do anything to get to the games, but he just didn't discuss them."

By today's standards, Plump didn't have much in his childhood. But he did have the things that mattered most in the fifties—friends, family, and sports. With those three, what else was really needed?

"I think life is always easier when you look back on it than when you're living through it," he says. "Life didn't seem very hard to me when I was growing up. Years probably have qualified that a little bit.

"My dad got two weeks of vacation every year, and some of the most pleasant memories I have are of those vacations. I looked forward to that more than I looked forward to playing in the state tournament. We always went down to Versailles State Park, about eight miles from Milan. In those days, there was a little creek that ran through there. Down by the power station there was a one-room shack that my dad rented every year from the state for two weeks. It leaked and we had to patch it. We had cots where we could sleep inside or outside. Pop Dunn, Glenn Butte, Fred Busching, Roger Schroder—there would be about five or six of us down there.

"This went on forever. We'd fish, swim, play cards. In that two-week period, a hundred people would drop in. The older guys would play penny ante, and we would play bottle-cap ante. God, that's been a long time ago. We had an old trailer, and we would load everything up in the trailer and just take off to the park."

119

Plump also spent much of those summers playing baseball and basketball, in his backyard or in the alley behind the Schroder store. In the beginning, Plump wasn't the star; he was just an average boy who played for the fun of it. Fun later turned to frustration when the talents of his friends progressed more quickly than his own. "In the sixth grade [Bob] Engel and [Ron] Truitt played on the seventh-and-eighth-grade team," he says. "I remember not being able to do that, and it was frustrating."

He practiced, practiced, and practiced some more, and Plump finally began to develop into a player. He played wherever he could find a ball. He developed his jump shot. He became quicker and stronger. The other things fell into place.

"I had gone to every basketball game I could go to ever since I was way down in the grades," Plump says. "A guy named Bill Gorman introduced the jump shot at Milan. In '49 and '50, they were still using and teaching the push shot. Then I saw Gorman shoot the jump shot, and I thought that looked like a good way to shoot. I copied him. I started doing that when I was a freshman."

He was ready when Snort Grinstead kicked seven seniors off the team in 1952 and made sophomores Plump and Bob Engel starters. They gave fans an indication of future greatness with a brilliant second half of the season. Then Plump missed the sectional with the flu. And when the season ended, Grinstead lost his job and Marvin Wood became the new coach.

Plump and Grinstead had developed a mutual respect for each other in that '52 season, and both had been eagerly awaiting the next season. Grinstead later told Lester Plump that his son was the best player he had ever coached. "When Grinstead was fired, I asked Roger Schroder if he thought I was going to be all right with the new coach," Plump says. "I just didn't have very much confidence."

But he could play. Plump was everything to those Milan teams in his junior and senior seasons. He didn't lead the team in scoring every game. He didn't grab many rebounds. He liked to stay away from the spotlight. But ask anyone who knew those teams, and you will hear that Plump held them together, that Plump made them go.

Plump scored thirteen points in the season-opening victory over Sunman, then hit double figures in virtually every game. He was the spark in the regional, scoring twenty-one of Milan's

120

fifty-three points against Morton Memorial, and then adding eight of Milan's twenty-four points in the championship win over Connersville. He scored ten and fifteen points in the two semistate games and sixteen in the season-ending loss to South Bend Central.

With a year of experience and maturity under his belt, Plump assumed a little bit bigger role. He averaged around twenty points a game in his senior season and was the closest thing to a go-to player that Milan had. For the second consecutive March, he turned his game up a notch for the tournament.

After a consistent sectional, Plump had a game-high sixteen points in the regional opener with Rushville. He followed that with twelve against Aurora in a game that saw Bob Engel and Ron Truitt take control late. The next weekend, on the Butler Fieldhouse floor in Indianapolis, Plump solidified his chances for the Mr. Basketball award. He had sixteen points in an afternoon victory over Montezuma, then scored twenty-eight in beating Indianapolis Crispus Attucks and sophomore sensation Oscar Robertson.

The game against Terre Haute Gerstmeyer in the state finals raised the eyebrows of those who had been asleep for the past year. Plump hit ten of fifteen field goals and added six free throws for a game-high twenty-six points. Said Kokomo *Tribune* sports editor Bob Ford, "His sparkling ball-handling and great teamwork had Gerstmeyer gasping several times."

"I loved it because I got to shoot a lot and score a lot," Plump said.

That performance against Gerstmeyer sent Plump blazing into what he hoped would be the greatest game in his career, against Muncie Central. It is the one that people remember, but it was by no means his best effort. He scored just five points in the first half, missing with the same regularity with which he had hit against Gerstmeyer. The second half wasn't much different: a free throw early in the third quarter, then two more late in the game.

That, of course, was all before he hit The Shot. It wasn't a lot different from the ones he had been missing the entire game, but it came at the perfect time in the perfect circumstance to forever link Plump to the miracle game. Forget about everything else, every other game. Plump and the miracle game go together like any blue-plate combination the Railroad Inn could ever serve.

"Fate works in a funny way," says Plump. "I had excellent games against Attucks and Gerstmeyer, and nobody ever talks about those games."

Just minutes after hitting The Shot to give Milan the team title, Plump won the coveted Trester Award for mental attitude and sportsmanship. A few weeks later, he learned he would wear the No. 1 jersey as Indiana's Mr. Basketball, leader of the Indiana All-Stars in their annual games with Kentucky's All-Stars. He had to take the announcement call at Schroders' store, because his family didn't own a telephone. Maybe Plump would have been Mr. Basketball if he hadn't hit that shot. His Attucks and Gerstmeyer games, his role in the two-year odyssey, had been noticed. The Shot guaranteed it.

"I really didn't know much about the all-star team," Plump said. "I knew it was something good, and I thought it was great. I don't remember thinking about an all-star game or thinking about being Mr. Basketball. It turned out to be a significant thing."

That was just the beginning of new things for Plump. He received mail from all over the country, including an Indian doll from a young girl. He still has five gallons of gas coming at a Shell Station in Goshen, 200 miles from Milan. He gained new pen pals from everywhere. The country boy from Pierceville was suddenly in demand to give speeches across the entire state. The self-described introvert spoke to students, athletes, clubs, and civic groups.

Several colleges across the country also desired his services, including Indiana, coming off two No. 1–ranked seasons and a national championship. It was never really a big contest because Plump knew he wanted to stay close to home, and the Butler program with Tony Hinkle was the logical choice. He knew the system after playing for Butler grad Wood, and he had a phenomenal record of success in Butler Fieldhouse.

Plump still keeps the handwritten recruiting letter from Hinkle in his desk drawer. It shows a simpler time, both in life and in college basketball. The letter, dated April 5, 1954, reads:

> Dear Bob,
> First may I congratulate [you] and your team mates on winning the I.H.S.A.A. championship. I probably got as big a kick out of it as you boys did.

Bob, I want you to come to Butler. We have a swell school and I know you will be satisfied here. We have a bunch of good boys. Also, I have a man who has taken an interest in you and wants to help you through school financially.
Some time when you get some free time, I want you to come up. I want to introduce you to the man and get your application for admission filled out.
Many schools probably will be after you, but just make up your mind to be with us. You can't go wrong.
When can you come up?

Sincerely,
Tony Hinkle

P.S. If any of the other boys want to come with you, bring them up also.

That letter and a subsequent campus visit apparently convinced Plump to attend Butler. "Facetiously, it was because the floor was good to me," he says. "Really, it was because of Mr. Hinkle and because of the schedule they played. I was familiar with the Hinkle system and thought I could play in that system. The larger schools scared me. You have to remember that I was extremely introverted except on the basketball court. That was a release to me."

Plump also says he never saw basketball as a way out of Pierceville, but he does admit he never would have attended college if not for his basketball talents.

"I asked my dad one time if I hadn't gotten a scholarship, would he have sent me to college," Plump recalls. "He said even if he had the money he wouldn't have. He said he didn't send the other kids to college so it wouldn't have been fair. I didn't look at basketball as a way out. I looked at basketball as something I was having a lot of fun at. It was not a means to an end. I don't remember playing basketball because I thought I could get out of here. I didn't think things were so bad. I wasn't necessarily looking to better myself."

After earning four varsity letters at Butler, Plump knew he had a shot at continuing his career. The NBA was a whole different world, nowhere near as attractive as now. An alternative some top stars of the era took was the National Industrial Basketball League, in which teams represented major industries that hired players to year-round executive positions and used them as players in winter competition. The Detroit Pistons—then the Fort Wayne Zollner Pistons—started that way. After his Butler years, Plump joined the best of the NIBL teams, the Phillips 66 Oilers of Bartlesville, Oklahoma.

Plump's chance with Phillips came after an East-West All-Star game in New York City. He had an offer to play with a college all-star team in an eighteen-game national tour against the Harlem Globetrotters. He would have received $1,800. He rejected that offer and flew to Oklahoma for a tryout with Phillips.

"They had never seen me play, had never seen a film," he recalls. "I shot for ten minutes, and they told me to take a shower. I saw $1,800 flying out the damn window. I thought, 'What did I do?' I took a shower, went into the office, and they said they wanted to hire me. I asked Bud Browning [coach of the 1948 Olympic team] later, 'How did you offer me the job when I just shot for ten minutes?' He said, 'While you were showering, I called Lou Wilkie, whom Mr. Hinkle had called. I told Lou the kid is quick and he can shoot but he's awful small. Lou said if Mr. Hinkle said he could play, hire him.' That's the reputation Mr. Hinkle had."

After that ten-minute tryout, Plump spent the next three years with the Oilers, who played exhibitions around the world in addition to their league schedule. He became an assistant coach after his three-year playing career, before taking the city sales manager's position in the company's Indianapolis office in September of 1963. He then switched to Fidelity Life Insurance, becoming a top representative through both his own hard work and the fact that he was as well known in Indiana as the governor.

Today, Plump, still active in insurance and financial planning, owns Bob Plump and Associates on Indianapolis's north side.

• • •

Gene White, the Milan center and Plump's Pierceville buddy, once joked that the only thing that would change if another small school won the state championship was that Plump would get fewer speaking engagements. In a more serious moment a few years ago, White composed a special poem for Plump on his fiftieth birthday, which hangs alongside Kyle Wright's poem in the office.

Bob Plump Is Fifty

He was so talented and shifty
That star guard of legend and fame
But now he has turned fifty
Insurance, not ball, is his game
Once opponents were made the fool
When into his gym they came
Now his best moves are from a stool
Upon which he espouses his fame
Tho we chide and generally spoof
This guy we call Bobby Gene
In Indiana, no place under roof
Will ever forget that player supreme
Now we gather to raise a toast
To his half-century birthday
And hear him make the boast
That he was the star, not Ray
Accept this ball and worn out shoe
Which ne'er more will be the same
As tokens to remind us and you
That the time clock doesn't stop in this game
                                    —Gene White

If anyone ever gracefully watched that clock wind down, it's Plump. He can live the past and the present at the same time. He likes interaction with people, and people like him.

He's still a legend in Indiana, and the movie put him in the national spotlight. There is no doubt that Plump would retain that legendary status even if some small school did win the title again. There comes a time when the legend becomes so big that nothing can overshadow it. Think Milan and you think Bobby Plump. Think Bobby Plump and you think Milan.

"Frankly, I've enjoyed it more the past ten years, winning the tourney and being more aware of everything," Plump says. "I'm very gratified that we're still talking about it. It's fun to talk about. It's more enjoyable to talk about. You can sit back and reflect on the years and enjoy it more now than you did back then."

Plump remains one of just three players to win the state championship, the Trester Award, and Mr. Basketball—Marion's Dave Colescott (who played at North Carolina in the 1970s) and Bedford's Damon Bailey (an Indiana University star of the '90s) the others. He was as sure a selection as Oscar Robertson or Johnny Wooden for the Indiana Basketball Hall of Fame, the highest honor for a basketball player in the Hoosier state.

But basketball does not dominate his life anymore. There are other things to do now before the clock finally winds down. "I thought many years ago that when I got forty-five or fifty, I would love to retire," he says. "I don't see myself retiring now. I enjoy what I do. I may slow down a little. I'm going to be doing the same things. It's a challenge to stay up with the new tax laws and the things that make our business exciting."

It's also the time of his life when Plump begins to wonder what kind of legacy he will leave. "I don't think I have any control over what people remember about me," he says. "I would like them to remember me as a pretty nice guy, somebody that had empathy for people and feelings, and that I had some impact on people that was positive."

10 *Bob Engel*

Bob Engel feels the time slipping away from him. His son, Chad, left for college two years ago, and his daughter, Shannon, graduated from high school in the spring of 1992. He was the last Milan player to have children graduate from high school, and he still tries to hold on.

"I can't get enough time with my kids," Engel says. "Those special times are precious and they're few and far between."

Engel is so self-conscious about his own children because his father left him, his mother, and his older brother and older sister just after he was born. The first time he saw his father was at the state tournament during his junior year. The elder Engel had evidently heard that his son was part of that miracle team making a run at the 1953 state title and decided it was a convenient time to come back into his life. "The only time he came to see me was during basketball, like to say, 'That's my son,' " Engel said. "You wonder why he didn't come and see me."

When his father died in Cincinnati in 1978, Engel didn't attend the funeral even though his brother and sister were there. He felt like it was someone he never really knew.

"My wife didn't understand that, and I told her it was because she always had a mother and father," he said. "To me, it was like going as a total stranger. It's water under the bridge, but I missed those things, a father giving you advice or telling you what direction to go. At that point in my life, something like that didn't bother me. I'd been that way from day one. I didn't have a father so it wasn't any big deal. Here you are, so you go on with your life. That's one of the things I'm not going to miss out on. I've tried to keep on top of those things with my son and daughter."

Engel sits in the kitchen of his modest one-story house in Portage, Michigan, just minutes from his job at the General Motors plant in Kalamazoo. It's in a quiet middle-class neighborhood with nice American cars in the garage and, of course, a basketball goal in the driveway.

He is pure middle-class, a self-described hard-working blue-collar laborer in an industry with a clouded future. The calories have caught up with him over the years, but he still looks good. His back still bothers him on occasion, and he rarely plays, but he can talk the best game of any player on that team. His story is the ironic twist to the miracle tale, because he was a genuine star-quality player whose part in the championship game was minimal, because of a bad back.

So maybe history and basketball don't remember him properly, but he remembers the sport, eloquently.

"I don't care if it was the county tourney, the sectional, the regional, or the state finals, you always had that same feeling of butterflies until you put that uniform on and stepped on that court and grabbed that roundball," he says. "Everything else was closed out."

Engel could also play a good game of roundball. Before he suffered that back injury his senior season, he was headed for a Division I scholarship. He was arguably the best player on that team.

"Engel may have been the best all-around athlete on the team," coach Marvin Wood says. "After the back injury, he couldn't run or jump, but he was a great shooter. He could shoot from thirty feet like he was shooting from fifteen. That's what people don't know. We won with one of our best players in ill health."

Says Rollin Cutter, "I think Bob was probably the best basket-ball player one-on-one that we had."

Says Plump, "I think Bob could have been as good as any player in that era if not for his back. The guy had raw talent. He could do anything. The one thing he lacked that would have held him back was quickness. He was an excellent shooter and one of the toughest competitors I've ever played with. He had a feel for the game and an intense desire to win."

Engel talks effortlessly for hours, part philosopher and part sentimentalist. His topics range from America's drug problem to Michael Jordan to the time he threw off his tie in that General Motors plant and went back to blue jeans and the assembly line. He talks often about sacrifice and dedication, characteristics he sees lacking in today's game. His ability to remember detail is amazing. He is the only player from that team who never attended college, yet in conversation he comes across as maybe the most educated of them all.

Milan has stayed with Bob Engel. It is embedded in him as much as that state championship. His mother still lives there, and he visits when time allows. He is a long way from Milan in miles, but so close in heart.

• • •

Engel grew up in downtown Milan, in an apartment above the beauty shop owned by his mother. He spent a lot of time with Ron Truitt, who shared a similar plight in life. He didn't have much, but he says he rarely thought about what might have been had the situation been different.

His mother earned a decent living by Milan standards, but it probably would have qualified on a poverty scale, if that era had had one. She spent as much time as possible in her beauty shop, trying to make a better life for her children. That often left Engel to take care of himself. It also left a lot of time for basketball.

He and Truitt went to the 1949 state finals with fellow Milan resident Carl Brown and sat two rows from the top as Jasper edged Madison for the title. After the game, Brown took them downtown to Kent Jewelers, where the state championship rings and trophies were on display. "He said, 'You know, if you boys work real hard, there's a possibility that someday you can get one of those,'" Engel recalls. "I had no idea we would get to that point."

Engel has a basketball story for every year, sometimes every day, of his childhood. As a kid, he delivered the Versailles *Republican* in Milan. There was rarely a day when he finished the route on time or didn't receive a customer complaint, because he usually got involved in a pick-up game. The problem was that the games were on the north end of town, and that was where Engel started his route. After a while, he switched and started from the south end so he could complete his route and then play in the games. He tells of coming home dead tired after practice and playing pick-up games with the neighbors using a portable light.

"We played basketball anytime, anywhere," Engel said. "If there was an old bushel basket hanging from a garage door, we were there. We loved the game. Two brothers lived next door. I'd come home from practice tired, and we'd still play. If we had a ball that didn't have enough air in it, we'd play anyway. When you have that roundball, you wanted to go on forever. There was no rush for anything. You just wanted to play, play, play."

Engel probably took the game more seriously than any of his teammates. He became one of the best shooters, he says, because of hard work and dedication. "You look back at the sacrifices you made," Engel says. "Today, everybody laughs at you. It falls back to the same things, the feelings you had for the game, the decisions you had to make. How many kids would go to bed at nine o'clock at night for one thing—to play that roundball?"

He says he went to bed every night at nine, not because Wood had that curfew but because he was so tired. It paid off in the 1952 season when Snort Grinstead kicked those seniors off the team and moved up Plump and Engel. Engel quickly found himself in the starting lineup of a team externally laden with talent and plagued by internal strife and did, in his own words, "very well."

Engel spent the summer after his sophomore year as a stock boy at Kroger to help meet his family's expenses. He saw Marvin Wood there one day, but he didn't know that the unimposing man, young but prematurely balding, was his next coach. "He came in the store and I didn't know who he was," Engel recalls. "Nothing on top, just around the edges. The manager knew who he was and came up after he left and said that was our new coach."

He worked that job and delivered papers because he had to, but

Engel played basketball because he wanted to. That was Indiana of the fifties. Nobody made anybody play basketball. They did it because they wanted to—and at least in Milan, maybe also because there wasn't much else.

Engel made an early impact on that '53 team, scoring thirteen points in the season opener against Sunman, then seven in the second game against Rising Sun. He played guard alongside Plump for most of the 1953 season and proved to be a versatile asset to the Indians.

He finished the regular season with a double-figures average but saved two of his best games for the semistate. Engel scored sixteen points in the 49–48 overtime win over Attica in the afternoon game at Butler Fieldhouse, and followed that with fourteen points in the championship against Shelbyville. A week later at the state finals, he hit just four of fifteen field goals and finished with seven points as South Bend Central ended Milan's season. That would also be Engel's last game at guard.

"He [Wood] came to me and asked if I would play forward," Engel says. "He said, 'You've got the fundamentals to play there.' I said, 'Fine, if it helps the team.' That summer I worked my butt off. If you followed me around that summer, you could have seen how much harder I worked."

Engel came back stronger than ever for that senior season. He could shoot, rebound, run the floor. Everyone who watched him knew he was headed for a college scholarship.

Just when Engel seemed at the peak of his high school career, his injury put everything in a different perspective. He says it was a practice in early December when he came across the lane, caught a pass from Craft, faked a shot, and then put up a left-handed hook. Glenn Butte bumped him when he was in the air, and Engel landed on his left side. Although he "felt something move," he wasn't too concerned about it at the time. By the next morning, however, it was obvious that something was wrong.

He still started, but he could not play with the intensity and stamina that had become his trademark during the past two years. Even with the injury, he was a potent scorer. He almost single-handedly ended favored Aurora's season in the Rushville Regional championship game with a seventeen-point performance, his high game of the season.

Engel, who scored just three points in an afternoon game

against Rushville, more than made up for it in the Aurora game. Milan trailed 27–20 at the half, and Engel had three fouls. He battled the foul trouble and helped the Indians rally in the second half while taking game-high scoring honors, but his biggest memory of the regional was of an old fan after the game.

"I can remember Duke Kohlmeyer standing under the basket after that game," says Engel. "He had a light beige jacket, a green tie, and green pants. He'd always walk under the basket before the game and he'd say, 'Engs, how you feel tonight?' He was standing there under the basket after the game. When I looked down and everyone else had left, there stood Duke Kohlmeyer, like he's lost, like he's gone. The sports jacket was draped over his arm, and so were his tie and shirt. He was standing there in his undershirt. He couldn't talk. He told me later, 'You came the closest of me having a heart attack as I've ever been in my life.' "

Perhaps the biggest urge to risk everything came at the state finals against Muncie Central when Engel started, played his few minutes, and then returned to the bench. The pain was so great by that time that he would not see any more action.

"I felt pretty secure when they taped me, but it was a lot of pain," he said. "I asked Mr. Morris [Jim, former Butler trainer] to give me a shot at halftime. He said, 'I won't do that for any athlete. I don't know what the condition of your back is. If I give you a shot for that pain and something else happens to you, I will never be able to live with that. You could wind up crippled or in a wheelchair.' "

So, in an unimaginable blend of pride and frustration, Engel watched from the bench as a dynasty that he had helped build defeated Muncie Central for the state title. "Even though I got to play in the first part of the game, I was really beside myself," he says. "Of all the time to be in that condition, it was the last game. This was it. There was no tomorrow."

He finished with two points in that game, a long set shot in the first half. He still feels he should have had two more points— officials didn't call an "obvious" foul when he went up for a first-quarter layup.

Even with the injury, Engel had several offers to play on the collegiate level, with the most interest coming from nearby Xavier and Cincinnati. "He had every opportunity to go to college," says longtime assistant Marc Combs. "UC [Cincinnati, which was to add Oscar Robertson two years later and become a national power] wanted him so bad."

Engel never attended a day of college. He never put a uniform on again, except for some city and recreational leagues.

"I was insecure about my physical condition," he says. "I still wasn't that confident. One thing I felt bad about was that after a couple of years, a lot of people were down on me because I didn't go to college. I can recall four or five people were all over me. They said, 'You had everything going for you. You could have been the best college basketball player.'

"But they forgot one thing. Financially, my mother was in no position to do it, and I wasn't going to be a burden on her. My mom could have put us in a foster home, but that didn't take place. I kept telling myself that I had to look ten years down the road. I didn't know what was going on with my back. That's why I chose to do what I did."

After graduating from Milan, Engel worked at an atomic energy plant in Hamilton, Ohio. He played in the city league there and had more offers to resume playing at the collegiate level. He turned those down, joined the army in 1958, and returned to the atomic energy plant three years later.

Engel attended an IBM training school and worked for that company several years before becoming the victim of a layoff in 1964. He married his wife, Cora, a year later, and they moved to Portage when a job opened at the new GM plant in Kalamazoo. He started in the factory, advanced to the position of supervisor, disliked that, and then returned to tools and maintenance.

It was during his early years in Michigan that Engel finally found a cure for his back ailment. Wood called him one day, asked if the back was still bothering him, and then told him to make a visit to see Jim Morris at Butler. What Morris discovered was that Engel's left leg was a quarter-inch shorter than his right leg. He put a quarter-inch lift in his left heel, and "two weeks later," Engel says, "I could do anything I wanted to do." Had he gone to Cincinnati and received similar treatment all those years before . . . who knows? He would have been a senior in 1958, Robertson's sophomore year, when UC just missed the Final Four—then made it the next five years.

Since graduating from Milan in '54, Engel has missed only

three championship reunions. He is several hundred miles away and all those years removed, but that team and the intangibles he received from that year are still part of him.

"If things like this happened early in your life, it has one big impact on how you live down the road," he says. "What's instilled in you at that point are things that you carry with you for the rest of your life. You can take this road or you can take that road. Those are decisions we were making at an early age, and that's helped me down the road. I've had no problems adjusting. A lot of the guys tell me, 'I wish I had the patience you've got.' Well, don't get in a hurry. Don't run over yourself."

One thing Engel does miss is being closer to his teammates. The distance often keeps him from attending other events, like the game against the team from *Hoosiers* at the opening of the Indiana Basketball Hall of Fame in New Castle.

He has become a transplanted folk hero in southern Michigan since the release of the movie. The local newspaper ran a page-one feature on him, and the area television station interviewed him at the plant for broadcast on the evening news. His friends now refer to him as "Hoosier."

There is talk that "Hoosier" will be an assistant coach at the local high school sometime soon. He attends all the games, and people often solicit his opinion about players and teams. He just might take that spot on the bench, with his own kids now in college.

"I told the guys up here, 'You want to talk about a spread offense? In 1954, we used a spread offense where you could drive a truck through the lane.' Somebody said it was too bad basketball didn't get the spark here like it does in Indiana. Up here, basketball is the secondary sport to football. I think it could come to be right up there. Football is the king up here. I wish I had the money because I would load up about three Greyhound buses and take these people one time to the state finals of Indiana basketball, and I guarantee you when they come back, they'll never stop talking about it."

• • •

Engel talks for a while and the philosopher begins to appear. He has the ability to analyze a situation, give a solution, and have everyone in the room believe him.

"All of these guys up here are asking me, 'Who was your superstar?' I tell them we didn't have one. That's why we won the state championship, because we won it together. We were all equal.

"The goosebumps are still there when you think about the guys and the sacrifices you made. That's what's wrong with today's superstars. A guy scores fifty points and he still gets beat. What's a superstar? He makes a lot of money, but how much do they win? Put your percentages on the table. Take your superstar, but if you don't have four other guys out there, you look kind of silly."

He talks about the Persian Gulf and wonders why America can't fight the drug problem with the same fervor. He talks about the school system and wonders where it is headed. He talks about the auto industry and wonders if it has any future at all. He talks often about young people and wonders about America's future.

"I think a lot of problems stem because parents don't listen to their children," he says. "You have to respect everybody's thoughts and input. Young people have a lot of good ideas, but the guy standing over here doesn't want to hear it. They want to turn the kids off. I don't like the way the system is going."

The hour grows late, and Engel disappears into the basement. He returns with a poster of the '54 schedule and advertisements of local businesses. The scores are written in with pencil. He looks intently at the poster and reflects about days gone by before speaking.

"I think it meant a lot to the town," Engel says. "It gave them something to talk about. To Milan, it was something. Guys didn't even know anything about the game and they were coaches. Now I'm looking at families and young adults starting their lives, and there's nothing in the town to bring them there. There's nothing wrong with growing up in a small town. The biggest problem is that at this point it would take a lot of turning around. It hurts to see the town like that, but what are you going to do? That's life."

The talk invariably returns to his kids and about that time slipping away. His son walks through the kitchen.

"He could have been a good ballplayer," Engel says. "Marvin Wood came up one time and they were out there shooting, and he asked why he wasn't playing. He loves baseball. I wasn't go-

135

ing to push him. If you like sports, I'll support you. If you have other interests, I'll support those."

His daughter walks through the same kitchen a little later. "One of the best pitchers in the league last year. It's just a matter of how bad she wants it."

He feels that time, time with his children, slipping away every minute, every second. He wants to freeze it, but he knows that would be impossible. Time marches on. He just needs to look at his hometown and his old teammates.

"There are times when you should say no, but the times today are so fast-paced that you can't say no," he says. "The kids are getting farther away from us. I want to feel like I've done everything I could possibly do to help them with what to expect out there in the real world. The things we want to do, we're running out of time to do them."

11 *Ron Truitt*

Think of every cliché and apply it to Ron Truitt. He was the glue that held the team together. He was the unsung hero. He preferred to stay out of the spotlight. His was a rags-to-riches story.

Ron Truitt probably had the least among a group of players that had very little. He was tough because he had no choice. On the basketball court, he could shoot, he could run, he could rebound, he could play defense.

"He could really go in streaks," says Bob Plump.

That was never more evident than in the 1954 regional final against Aurora. Truitt picked up three fouls in the first half, and the Indians trailed 27–20. He hit the two key baskets in a second-half spurt that gave Milan a spot in the Sweet Sixteen. He tied the game at 34 with a long field goal, then hit another just seconds later to push Milan into the lead for good at 37–36.

But the story of Ron Truitt goes far beyond that of a basketball court, maybe farther than the tale of any player on that '54 team.

Walter "Peck" Truitt was Ron's father and the closest thing Milan had to Dennis Hopper's "Shooter" character in the movie

Hoosiers. There was one big difference. Peck Truitt liked to drink, but he never bothered anyone. He didn't attend the games, and he certainly never sat on the bench as an assistant coach. "He could really pick a guitar," says Bob Engel. "If he hadn't gotten in that bottle, he would have done all right. He never made a scene. He never came on the floor."

Ron Truitt wanted to be a basketball player even before he attended the '49 finals with Engel and Carl Brown. People took care of Truitt. That's just the way it was in a small town. No one bothered him about his father. No one probably even thought to do it.

"After a while, the people respected Ronnie enough to let it go," says Engel. "They thought he had enough problems the way it was. Ron took it in stride. It never upset him much because he had been faced with this from day one."

Truitt certainly didn't have many problems on the basketball court. He was good enough to start his junior season in '53 and was usually good for anywhere from six to ten points a game. He played a bigger role during his senior season, which was highlighted by that performance in the Rushville Regional.

"He was probably a better basketball player than he got credit for," says Plump.

He attracted several scouts, but it was obvious he couldn't afford to pay even minimal costs at college. The situation changed when Houston, with a young Guy Lewis as coach, made its visit. Truitt's sister lived in the area, and he could save housing costs if he lived with her. Basketball would take care of the tuition.

The one with the least went farther away than any other senior on the team.

"Ron was probably the one guy who didn't get many breaks," says Rollin Cutter. "His biggest break was playing basketball at Milan and getting an opportunity to leave and go to Houston. That's where he blossomed. He was a nice kid. He just didn't have a very good background. He really got a good break from this experience."

As it turned out, Truitt never really went back to Milan. He graduated from Houston, found a coaching position in Texas, married, and had two kids. He also found success where the other members of that championship team failed. Unlike any of his former teammates, Truitt coached a team that won a state basketball championship.

He visited Milan for the usual occasions; he even made a reunion every once in a while. When *Hoosiers* hit the big screen in 1987, Truitt returned to his roots. He attended the big party with the other players and rode in the Cadillacs to see the film in Batesville. It seemed like old times again.

It was also the last time Truitt would see his teammates.

Ron Truitt died about a year later from cancer. The irony of the story was that no one from that '54 team, including Wood, knew that Truitt had the disease. He just went on with life as usual, not even telling anyone at the premiere of the movie just a year before he died.

Bob Engel counts himself as Truitt's best boyhood friend. He says they were inseparable as kids. Engel learned of Truitt's death by telephone just a few hours before the Houston funeral.

"I thought about it a lot after he passed away," says Engel. "It hurt because we were close, like brothers. No one had any indication of any sort. He said he hadn't been feeling good, but he let it go at that. He was always the unsung hero. He was always there and giving support, but he didn't ever want to be in the front row. When I went down there to visit him once, it was like old times. I think he wanted out. I think he wanted to come back."

Says Ray Craft, "Ron Truitt knew he had cancer [when he last came to Milan]. When he said he needed to get away and visit his grandmother or something like that, I wonder if that wasn't the reason. He probably had less and achieved more than anybody."

Truitt also had a special relationship with longtime junior high coach Marc Combs. Combs had kept a watchful eye on Truitt as he progressed through the grades. Truitt had always returned the respect.

"He was one of the nicest guys you would want to meet," says Combs. "He paid me a great compliment that I've never felt worthy of. The last thing he ever said to me was, 'Marc, I owe everything I am to you.' That's when you start to cry. Those are the things that pay for all of the hard work you put into it. I told Ron, 'You don't owe anybody anything. You did it on your own. You worked at it.' "

Hard work is what most people remember about Truitt. People remember that in Milan and they remember it in Houston. He worked hard enough to make the high school team, worked hard enough to make it through college in Houston, and worked hard enough as a coach to win a Texas state championship at Cy-Fair High School in the 1970–71 season.

After a successful coaching stint, he became the assistant principal and later assumed the role of principal. He made such a contribution to the Houston area and such an impact on the lives of those associated with the school that the district now has Truitt Junior High School, named in his honor less than a year after his death. No other Milan Indian, not even Plump, has a school named for him.

"He was a very loyal person," remembers Ken Pridgeon, a colleague of Truitt's in Houston. "He was a team man. In his coaching, he was loyal to his team and his athletes."

And even in Houston, far removed from Indiana farmland, the people didn't forget that Truitt helped inspire a movie. Pridgeon remembers that more than 400 people jammed a Houston auditorium for a preview of *Hoosiers* and gave the surprised guest of honor a hero's welcome. Pridgeon, who saw Truitt on a daily basis, says that it was difficult to realize that he was terminally ill. "He didn't ever talk about it," Pridgeon says. "He didn't want anybody's sympathy. Yeah, we all thought a lot of Ronnie Truitt."

Maybe more than anything else, the Milan players still struggle with the death of Ron Truitt. It used to be that he lived in Texas, but there was the possibility that he would come back on occasion. They could always reach him on the telephone. Now they know he can't come back.

Maybe it's the realization that one of their age has died. Maybe it's the fact that he drifted away from most of his teammates when he moved to Texas.

Or maybe it's just as Gene White says it is.

"It was just too early to die," says White. "That was the problem."

12 *Gene White*

It's almost funny now, when Gene White thinks back on it. It was the early eighties, and White was coaching the boys' varsity basketball team at Milan High School, his alma mater. Girls' basketball was just getting started at Milan, and the coach of the boys' team made it known who was in charge.

"I was really tough on the girls at Milan," White recalls. "They were not very good. Because of the way they approached the game, I thought they were in the way of the boys. I was mean to them unintentionally. If they wanted the floor, I wouldn't let them on it."

Less than ten years later, women's basketball is a big part of White's life. He coaches the Franklin College women's team after years of boys' high school basketball.

His professional life has followed that of his old Milan coach, Marvin Wood. He enjoys looking back at the numerous achievements in his high school coaching days, but he's happy with his current life. "I think Gene is a better person for having been around Marvin," says White's mother, Genevieve, who still lives in Ripley County. "Right off, Marvin let everyone know who the boss was, and he was a good moral person."

White has gone through life like a ping-pong ball. He keeps bouncing back and forth between the two places he loves. He played and coached at Milan. He played and is coaching at Franklin College.

His life is much more relaxed in the nineties. He wants to win, but there is little pressure from administrators to pile up the victories. It's not like the days when he coached at Milan, when people expected him to recreate that miracle of '54.

And somewhere in the shuffle, White discovered that women can also play the game. He found they are coachable and want to learn. He found that after taking away the crowds and the history of Indiana boys' basketball, the actual games remain very similar.

"From all aspects except the physical playing of the game, there are no differences," White says. "The things we try to do here are the same things I taught the boys. We run the same offenses and the same defenses. I don't think the size of the crowd is a factor to me. I can block those things out. Even when I played, I could ignore crowds and bands."

He has not been able to ignore the spotlight in the post-championship years. Many of his players' fathers remember watching that Milan–Muncie Central game when they were young. He contends that isn't a major recruiting tool, but it certainly can't hurt.

White has a full beard and glasses now. The calories have started to stick with him. He says he can still run on a basketball court, but not forever as in days gone by. He did play against the cast of *Hoosiers* at the grand opening of the Indiana Basketball Hall of Fame in 1990. "When Plump called me, I didn't think I could get up and down the court," White says. "We played about ten minutes and did all right. We were bigger than they were, so we put it on them. We were old, but that doesn't mean that you can't shoot the basketball. It just means that you can't run as much and can't play defense."

White and Bob Engel are the sentimentalists from the '54 team. The championship seems like a bigger accomplishment as White grows older and more reflective. He calls his teammates the closest group to ever play the game of basketball. He really believes it.

"As the days mount up, its meaning gets greater," he says. "Every old person looks back on their childhood fondly. When you have a highlight like that, it tends to make you a little closer."

• • •

The house where Gene White would be living had Milan not won that state title in 1954 is just on the outskirts of Pierceville. It's a typical farmhouse—white, two-story, big porch. There are ten acres of land, not much by farming standards. White's parents farmed that land and operated a feed mill near the railroad tracks in the heart of Pierceville. They didn't fill the town bank with their farming profits, but they made enough for a decent life.

His childhood story is much like that of Pierceville buddies Bob Plump, Roger Schroder, and Glenn Butte. He worked a lot for his parents, and he played a lot of sports. Baseball and basketball were his true loves. He became good because there just wasn't anything else to do. "Back then, you didn't go anywhere," he says. "We didn't have a lot of money and we didn't have a car. If we went to Milan on a Saturday night, that was a big social event. We looked forward to those Saturday nights."

It was obvious early in his basketball career that he would be the big man. It wasn't that he was huge—just 6-1—but he was taller than the other Milan players. "We put him in the middle of the zone in elementary school," says junior high coach Marc Combs. "He was the general on defense. He was the center of that zone. He talked to everybody, told everybody what to do."

White's mother says there was a time when she thought her son was too big. "Gene was a little heavy and I thought he moved too slow," she recalls.

She quickly learned otherwise. White never really developed into a superstar, but most agree that Milan would not have had the same degree of success without him. He clogged the middle on defense, pulled down the big rebounds, and scored when the team needed him.

He spent his summers like everyone else, working a little bit at the family feed mill and playing basketball in Schroders' driveway. It was a good life for a kid, no big-town hassles, no waiting to play a pick-up game, no pressure from anybody.

White won a starting spot his junior season. He was listed at an even six feet in the programs and played forward opposite Ron Truitt, with Jim Wendelman in the middle. He also scored his share of points, hitting for sixteen against Brookville, fourteen against Osgood, and twelve each against Holton, Sunman, and North Madison. His best game in 1953 came when he knew he needed to turn in a good effort. With Plump and Jim Wendelman sidelined for breaking the team curfew, White scored a season-high nineteen points in a victory over Napoleon.

Even with his stellar junior season, White still was not assured of a starting spot for his senior year. There was Bob Wichman, who was hurt just before the tourney. There was Rollin Cutter, a tall junior who could play either forward or center. There was Glenn Butte, just a sophomore but good enough to start on many area teams.

Here was a team that had gone to the state finals and still had more talent than most of the other county squads combined. And White was right in the middle of what could be called a "talent glut," if such a thing exists.

"There was always a guy breathing down my neck for my job," White says. "There was a lot of pressure, and that was in practice."

White did earn and keep his spot for the entire season. With Jim Wendelman gone, White moved to center. Once again he became the general on the defensive end of the court. He wasn't really intimidating at 6-1, but he got the job done. He helped dictate the tempo for a team that relied on tempo as much as anything else.

White was also the team spokesman, the intellectual on the team, and reporters often sought him out for interviews. "I don't think any seventeen- or eighteen-year-old kid gets tired of it ever," White says.

His mother had a different theory. She worried about her son getting caught up in the hype and not concentrating on the game. She preferred that he come home and play a quiet game of canasta as opposed to talking to reporters. "I ran reporters off," she says. "Those boys were just kids, and I wasn't about to let some reporter cause Gene's head to swell. I just wouldn't let them talk to Gene. He still doesn't know that. You have to do a lot of things in certain situations. Kids start to believe a lot of things that are written about them, and I couldn't have that."

If she did indeed shield her son from the media, it was a good move. White's name was always in the box score, but he was rarely the team leader in scoring. In fact, he was the high-point man in just one regular-season game, when he scored fourteen points in a 36–30 victory over county rival Napoleon.

But on defense, he was Milan's heart and soul. That was most evident in the 1954 regional final with Aurora, when he matched up against Bob Fehrman, a potent scorer who had hit for twenty-three points when Aurora had defeated Milan 54–45 in the regular season. He was coming into the regional game on an even bigger roll after scoring thirty-five points, a regional record, against Connersville in the afternoon round. White held Fehrman to four field goals—all in the first half—and twelve total points.

It's still a game that White cherishes, not just because of what he did on defense but also because it was Aurora. This was a team that was geographically close to Milan, a team that had handed the Indians one of only two defeats in the regular season. "That game was our crowning achievement," says White. "They were probably as good as Muncie. They were close to us, so it was an even bigger game than Muncie."

The championship game against Muncie Central is the perfect example of White's importance to the team. He scored just one point, but watch the tape and he's there at every big play, getting a rebound, cutting someone off at the baseline.

Ironically, the play that stands out in his mind is the one that he didn't make. "When they tied the score at 30, I thought I could have blocked the shot or fouled the guy," he said. "I was in a position where I didn't react quick enough. I thought I could have gotten to him."

White, salutatorian of the Milan class of 1954, was definitely the team's intellectual member. When the team gathered for a pep session, he was always the designated speaker. He recalls, "In those days, guys weren't very good at talking. At the pep sessions, it was usually twelve guys saying I hope we win. Afterwards, it was probably twelve guys saying I'm glad we won."

White was bound for Purdue to study agriculture back in the winter of 1954. Go to college, become one of the few people in the county with a degree and come back to make a fortune—or at least a respectable living—on the family farm. That was the plan. Until, of course, that game changed the world.

"He was all set to study some sort of agriculture at Purdue," his mother says. "After they won the tournament, it changed everything."

Franklin College replaced Purdue. Mathematics replaced agriculture. Teaching and coaching replaced farming.

"It had a big effect, being on that team," White says. "It educated me literally. There was the question mark about how many of us would have gone to college. Maybe I would have and maybe I wouldn't have. In the 1950s, you could make money in your immediate environment without a college education."

But White also had the foresight to know that there was a distant, as well as immediate, future. He knew, maybe more so now when looking back on everything, that there was life outside Milan. The state championship educated him that life existed away from Pierceville and the family feed mill.

He received an academic scholarship to Franklin and played two years of varsity basketball before deciding his future was in coaching instead of shooting and defending. After graduating from Franklin, he spent two years in the army and the following seven years coaching at Batesville, the old Milan rival that had knocked the Indians out of the sectional tourney four straight years in the early fifties.

Then White made the decision to go home. Thomas Wolfe said you can never go home again. Probably, Gene White is now a believer.

The situation looked like a heavenly match in the newspapers. Here was the local boy, the one who had helped give his hometown the proudest moment in its history, the one who went off to college in pursuit of a higher education, the one who had decided to finally come home and make his old school a winner once again.

That was the fairy-tale version. The real-life story didn't quite go according to those lines.

White coached at Milan from 1982 to 1985. He tried to fit right back into the "one of us" mold again. He visited the old stomp-

146

ing grounds, had the same barber trim his hair, even served on the town board in attempts to pump some life back into Milan.

When he took over the program, people began to whisper that he could bring back the magic of thirty seasons past. He never hid the fact that he was part of that championship squad. In fact, Plump jokes that White may have even stretched his role a little too far. "I went down there for a game," Plump recalls, "and one of the players said, 'Mr. Plump, can you show us how Mr. White hit that final shot?' "

Probably to the disbelief of the few realists in the town, White did turn the team's fortunes around. He capped the reversal with a sectional championship in 1985, and the ball rests today in the trophy case near the main entrance of the high school. But this time, the road ended much earlier when the Indians lost in the regional. Given the success of Milan when White took over the program, that sectional victory should have been lauded as an incredible accomplishment.

Times had changed. Teams had changed. For Milan merely to capture the sectional again was something just short of a miracle. But White had been part of that once-in-a-lifetime team, and the people wanted him to perform another magic show.

"We did have a decent ballclub and we did win the sectional," White says. "Then the comparisons started. As soon as Milan wins the sectional, there are people who want to say you can do things you can't really do. We weren't that good. I felt like we could do a little better."

After his sectional championship season, White ran into the roadblock that has ended many coaching careers: conflict with the administration. "The administration was going through some changes," he said. "I disagreed with some of those. I had a little falling out with the educational theory at Milan. I finally said I could do the same thing somewhere else. So I left."

He returned to Franklin, but at the high school instead of the college, to teach math and serve as assistant coach to the girls' basketball team. The collegiate vacancy opened shortly after Milan resident Jenny Johnson, the softball player of the city limits sign, became the women's athletic director at Franklin College. White seemed the logical choice to Johnson, and he needed little coaxing to take the job despite the fact that the school offered no athletic scholarships.

"When I came, they had a good ballclub," White says. "Unfortunately, many of them were seniors. As a new coach, I never thought we got the most out of them as ballplayers. The next year, we did better with less talent." The team's records have stayed around .500. "Against the teams that give scholarships, we don't do very well," White said.

Now White teaches summer school at the college and someday hopes that he can become a full-time member of the Franklin faculty. "I've almost accomplished what I wanted to," he says. "I played at Milan and then coached there and did as well as I thought I could. Then I came back here. I don't have any ambitions to go to another school."

• • •

It was one of those games you hate to win and you hate to lose. It was the coach against the student. It was a chance to show what you had learned, but it was also a time to show respect. It was White versus Marvin Wood, Franklin College versus Saint Mary's.

Here was a study in similarity between two men whose careers had followed such parallel paths. They had coached a lot of teams, but they had never sat on opposing benches. For a couple of games at least, they were now opponents. It wasn't a war, but it was a big deal.

The teams met once in 1989 and again in 1990. It ended appropriately—a split. "It was a little incentive for me," said White. "I told the girls last year [1990] that we wanted to run them. He did exactly the same thing to us. We're very similar in our styles and how we approach the game."

White still brings the same attitude with him from the high school classroom to the college gymnasium. It's one he developed playing on that goal at Schroders' old store. It's one he perfected at Milan, Franklin, Milan again, and now Franklin again. It's the same Gene White, just a little older, a little wiser.

His office just off the gymnasium at Franklin College isn't big, but it's enough. He comes there every day after teaching a full day of math at Franklin High School. He's usually there by 4:00 P.M., even in the off-season. He has a future to plan, more games to win. There's always work when your philosophy is that one loss is too many.

"I'm one of those win-every-one guys," he said. "We're out to win every game. We don't have the goal of the national tourney. If we win enough games, we'll get there. The girls here play hard. I've always thought you play against perfection. What we want is perfection. We may never achieve it, but that's what we want.

"Sports is like dancing. You want to look good when you're dancing. I don't ever consider something an impossible task. I think it's a cop-out to say that we can't play with that school because they give scholarships and we don't. When we approach a game, we don't let that get involved. I can truthfully say, with very few exceptions, that we don't think we're going to get beat. That's Milan coming through.

"I tell the girls the same thing my dad told me: 'Those girls are nineteen or twenty just like you. Should they be that much better than you?' When the kid is that much taller than you, why should you say that he's that much better?"

13 *Ken Wendelman*

Excuse Ken Wendelman if the importance of winning the state title in 1954 has diminished for him over the years. He's had a lot of other things on his mind.

Wendelman, who rarely, if ever, returns for any of the championship reunions, has endured more situations in the past thirty years than most people would in about five lifetimes. He has been near death twice, suffered through two other painful illnesses, and had a personal life not exactly filled with joy.

"I've been through a lot," Wendelman said.

When he was just twenty-nine, Wendelman had cancer of the lymph nodes. "I was supposed to die from that," he says. "They took a hunk out of me that looked like a piece of beef. The doctor told me on the tenth anniversary when I was thirty-nine, 'I don't know why you've lived. You were supposed to be dead by now.' "

When he was in his early forties, Wendelman was diagnosed with Bell's Palsy, a condition that results in partial paralysis of the face. It's treatable, but he admits, "That will never be right."

Just a few years later, Wendelman realized he had skin cancer, his second cancer in twenty-five years. Then, in May of 1991, he suffered a heart attack. "It was a real good one," he says. 'I'll never be the same after that either. I guess everybody gets old."

Wendelman is able to keep a surprisingly upbeat perspective despite the setbacks. About the best explanation he can rationalize is that life throws some curves along the way.

"I've been through some stuff," he says. "But all you can do is keep on kicking. You don't give up. I learned that from Woody and my mom and dad. You just don't quit."

That's about the easiest way to say it. Ken Wendelman has seen tough times. He lives alone in Versailles after a divorce several years ago. His mentally handicapped son, Robert, named after former Milan teammate Bob Engel, lives in a nearby group home.

Perhaps the best example of Wendelman's will is in his work. Despite the heart attack, he keeps a busy schedule. He still operates Wendelman Construction in his hometown of Versailles, just a short drive from Milan. He says he still enjoys putting in a full day of work.

He has lived in the area since, in his own words, "day one." His mother, now in her late eighties, lives in Milan. His brother, Jim, drives a truck in nearby Batesville, and his sister, Rita, also still lives in the area.

"I've had chances to go other places, but I didn't," he says. "It's surprising to me that you can go anywhere and people still ask about Milan. They really don't talk about it that much around here [Versailles] anymore. It might come up on television, and you're sitting in a bar and people ask you about it. As far as every day or every week, it's not talked about. Maybe they still do it in the Milan coffee shop but I don't make it over there much."

Partly because of his busy schedule and partly because of his work, Wendelman usually stays away from the reunions and other activities involving the '54 team. He did attend the thirtieth-anniversary reunion, but for the most part he's his own man.

Wendelman does brag that he was quite an athlete in his day—a 200 bowling average, a scratch golfer, a good arm and a decent hitter in baseball, a standout on the track team. He still holds the Milan long-jump record at twenty-one feet, eight inches.

He realizes what it meant, and still means, to be a part of that championship Indian team. He also realizes that there comes a time when what's over is over. You can't live on past accomplishments forever.

"It was a good experience," he says. "You don't trade it for anything. But I don't eat, sleep, and drink it like I used to. It's history for me. It won't make me any money and it won't break me. I'm not saying it doesn't mean anything now, but I don't get up every day looking forward to being interviewed or talking about things that happened in 1954. That's just not my bag."

• • •

Ken Wendelman grew up on a 120-acre farm outside Milan with his brother and sister. His parents, Irven and Myrtle, farmed the land, and his father also worked at the Seagrams plant between Pierceville and Milan. That left a lot of the farm work for the two brothers.

"I was just an old farm boy, a real exciting life," Wendelman jokes. "I worked hard. I worked every night, every weekend, every summer. I worked in the morning before I went to school doing chores. We weren't ever rich, but we were in good shape."

Baseball, not basketball, was always Wendelman's game of choice. He remembers a love for baseball before he ever remembers playing basketball at all. In fact, he didn't try out for the basketball team until his junior year. He was already at a big disadvantage because most of his teammates had been playing since the second and third grades.

"I just wanted something to do, I guess," he says. "If you lived on a farm back in those days, you had to work. You didn't have time for other things. Other guys were playing all the time. I wasn't out there that much. I probably didn't have the confidence of a lot of the other guys because it was my first year. The other guys had been playing all the way up through grade school."

Joining the team turned out to be a good move because that was Marvin Wood's first year and the Indians advanced to the Final Four. Wendelman spent the season playing two quarters for the junior varsity and then dressing for most of the varsity games.

There was some friendly competition in the Wendelman

household that season since Ken's brother, Jim, served as Milan's starting center. It was Jim Wendelman who set the tone for that semistate victory over Shelbyville with his intimidating and dominating inside play.

Jim Wendelman wasn't the reason that Ken decided to play, but having him on the team did help.

"For his day, Jim was big, about 6-3 or 6-4," says Ken. "He could handle himself underneath and he was a good rebounder. Once I went out, there was some competitiveness between us. I still say I was a better athlete."

In retrospect, what seems remarkable is that Wendelman made it to the state finals in just his first season of organized basketball. True, he wasn't one of the standouts, but he was good enough to make a talented team. He still finds that year difficult to believe.

"Making it to Butler Fieldhouse was the biggest thing around," he says. "That was quite a trip. Once you're there, you think you can make it back. You're a lot smarter."

Wendelman knew he would play a bigger part in his senior season. He describes his role on that Indian team as a ball chaser on defense, a backup to center Gene White, and an occasional starter. He also picked up some more responsibility, along with Rollin Cutter and Glenn Butte, when Bob Engel suffered his back injury midway through the season.

The biggest moment of the season for Wendelman—and the biggest moment of his career—came in the championship game against Muncie Central. He was on the floor when the game was won. He replaced Cutter with about three minutes remaining, mostly for his quickness on defense and his rebounding abilities. In the final sequence before Plump hit the game-winning shot, Wendelman was in the left-hand corner with the other three Indian players.

"I can't really recall what I was thinking," he says. "I just headed for the basket when he shot it. We didn't have to worry about the rebound. That's about all there was to it."

A couple of days later, Wendelman's picture appeared in two out of every three newspapers across the state—sitting with Ray Craft on the hood of the lead Cadillac, the championship trophy between them, returning with the team to Milan.

But Wendelman's high school athletic story doesn't end there. His sport was baseball, and that season didn't begin until spring.

153

No one kept baseball records like they did in basketball, and the state didn't have a high school baseball tournament until 1965, but Wendelman says that Milan team was one of the best in the state. Wendelman was so confident of his abilities that he attended a tryout camp with the Cincinnati Reds at old Crosley Field.

"I had a chance to go to Tampa with them for spring training," he says. "That was after graduation. But my parents wanted me to go to college, so I went to college."

Wendelman enrolled at Franklin College along with teammate Gene White. He majored in physical education and minored in biology. He had hoped to become a teacher. He didn't play any varsity sports at Franklin, but says he averaged thirty points a game in the intramural basketball league.

His initial goal of teaching ended abruptly when he dropped out of Franklin after his junior year. "I just quit," he says. "I just wasn't into it. There were things I would rather do then than go to school."

Wendelman returned to his roots and took a job in construction that would later turn into a career. He worked ten years for a small company and started Wendelman Construction in the late sixties.

He says the business today is both busy and successful. He also says he rarely looks back on what might have been had he completed that fourth year of college at Franklin.

"I've got a good job," he says. "I make good money. Another year of college wouldn't have taught me any more than I know now. The way life has turned out for me, it wouldn't have helped me. I'm doing what I like to do. I'm single, so my life is my work, playing a little golf, and doing a lot of fishing."

He's grown up and endured a lot over the years, but in a lot of ways Wendelman remains that old farm boy that he described in the beginning.

• • •

If there's one regret for Ken Wendelman, one thing that he thinks could have been different about his life, it's that tryout with the Cincinnati Reds. Who knows what could have happened had he gone to Tampa with the Reds that spring instead of going to Franklin College? A second invitation never came because Wendelman injured his arm the next year while playing in a variety of fast- and slow-pitch leagues.

"I know I had a chance," he says. "You never know what could have happened. Basketball wasn't as important to me as baseball. That was my game. I was a good baseball player, a lot better at baseball than at basketball."

But Wendelman is remembered as a basketball player because his team won the state title. He also lives closer to Milan than any other player from that team. All that makes for an inevitable link between Wendelman and the title.

Most of his former teammates say they wish Wendelman would attend the reunions more frequently, that he's a classmate as well as a teammate. Wendelman answers that he "can't be everywhere." Some things just don't work out like they should.

Though he doesn't live the championship anymore, Wendelman has not totally distanced himself from the event and the team. He says he maintains regular contact with Gene White and talks on occasion with Bob Engel—the friend and teammate after whom Wendelman named his son.

"Bob and I were good friends," he says. "When you're in school, you may play ball with a group, but there are one or two you're close to. Engel and White were the ones I was close to."

Life probably won't change much for Wendelman in the next few years. The odds are that he can't go through many tougher situations than he has already endured. He looks forward to his work every day, even though the heart attack has forced him to cut back somewhat. He says he will work as long as he can and then retire to a life of golf and fishing.

And somewhere he will maintain a part of his experiences on that team of teams. He probably won't attend any more reunions, but it will always be with him.

"It had to mean something to you," he says. "Not everyone can do it. It's like winning a World Series. People play all their careers and don't accomplish what others do in one year. It does mean more to some than to others. I don't attend all the gatherings. I've got a busy life.

"I'm not into the limelight. I don't get into it. Even sports today, some people like to get on TV and some of them don't. There are different personalities. That's all it is. I do what I do and I did what I did. It's no big deal."

14 *Ray Craft*

Ray Craft, the shy and soft-spoken guard, is probably the quietest player from that '54 Milan team. At least that's how he appears on the surface.

He answers any questions about the miracle run, but it usually takes three questions to get a one-sentence response. It's obvious that he doesn't like to brag about his past achievements, although he has a portfolio that could fill a book, or at least one of those lengthy magazine articles. Everyone from his former teammates to the current Milan residents calls Craft the shiest member of that squad.

Craft was also a leader on that team. Says former teammate Rollin Cutter, "Ray is a real quiet guy. To see him play basketball and to see him today, you would think it was two different guys. He was a real sparkplug, very aggressive."

He also rarely receives much of the credit for Milan's success. When Bob Plump hit that last-second shot in the final game against Muncie Central, Craft was destined to be in the shadows forever.

What most people don't know is that Craft had an opportunity just seconds earlier to seal a Milan victory. The Indians had a 30–28 lead and the ball with just over a minute remaining in the game. Craft broke loose for what seemed to be a game-clinching layup, but the ball rolled in—and out. The Bearcats scored, and then Plump hit the game-winning jumper just seconds later.

Says Plump, "He was a better basketball player than he got credit for, perhaps because of the last shot I hit."

Craft has used being a member of that team in his climb to assistant commissioner of the Indiana High School Athletic Association. He might have made it without that championship ring, but having it certainly never hurt. Winning that state title gave Craft the biggest push in his quest to become a coach and then an administrator.

"When we won it, Marvin Wood said it wasn't that big of a deal," says Craft. "The longer it goes, it seems like it is a big deal. Maybe I'm more amazed the longer it goes and the longer it lives. This many years after it, people still talk about Milan.

"We knew basketball was big in Indiana, but we weren't old enough to realize the effect it would have. I've always realized the importance it had on my life and my future. It's something I'm very proud of and I'm happy to be a part of it. I would never push the subject on someone, but if someone wants to talk about it, I always will. I'll never get tired of it."

As he grows older and the game grows bigger, he also realizes the importance of keeping in touch. He thinks back to the 1990 reunion in South Bend, when he missed the Friday night session because of the state baseball tourney in Indianapolis. He knows those are times that can't be made up.

"I should have gone up there on Friday night," he says now. "With one having died and one having cancer, it's more important to go back every year. You are at that stage where things can happen. At our age now, it's just that we survived another year. It's great that this type of thing can keep us coming back year after year. I still feel pretty close to some of the people. If anybody needed help, we would be there."

It's the team that Craft talks about, from the actual championship game against the Bearcats to the last reunion. The team did this. The team did that. The team won at a team sport. One look at the old clippings would show that Craft was a standout as an individual, but years have put that in perspective. He prefers that

157

the spotlight shine on all ten players, not just a select few because they scored the most points or grabbed the most rebounds.

"We didn't get wrapped up in the scoring and all of that," says Craft. "We had no jealousies on the team. We worked together as a team. The most important thing was winning. We didn't keep statistics like they do today. It just wasn't the way it is today."

• • •

Ray Craft is the only player on the 1954 Milan team who was not a native of Ripley County. He was born in Middletown, Ohio, and moved to Milan with his parents when he was in the fourth grade. His parents bought an eighty-acre farm just north of Milan, plenty of room for their seven children. He and Rollin Cutter were the two farm boys who would later walk home after each varsity practice.

Even though he was just in the fourth grade, Craft could already notice the sports differences between Ohio and Indiana. People in the Buckeye state just didn't get as excited about roundball as they did in the Hoosier state. He could never have foreseen the path he would someday take, but he did notice there was a certain aura about Indiana high school basketball. He knew that he liked sports, but he couldn't have known the success he would eventually enjoy.

"I didn't have much of a feel for basketball in Ohio," he says. "We were a farm family, and my parents weren't really sports-oriented."

That didn't keep Craft from choosing the basketball over the tractor. He played on the junior varsity during his sophomore season, then moved to the varsity as a reserve when Wood became coach the following year. He played behind Plump and Engel most of the '53 season, but did contribute in most games.

When Engel moved to forward the next fall, it seemed that Craft would inherit the starting guard spot. Wood had other ideas. In the first game, Wood chose to start Bill Jordan at guard and use Craft off the bench as the sixth man. That tactic worked in the victory over Rising Sun, but it also lasted just one game. Wood permanently inserted Craft into the starting lineup.

"I think Marvin liked the idea of somebody like that coming off the bench," Craft says. "He then thought it was unfair to me. If I was good enough to start, then I should get the opportunity."

158

In retrospect, it seems like a wise decision. Craft teamed with Plump to form a potent guard combination. He could handle the ball and find the open man, or he could pull up and take the jumper. There was no way that a team could key on either Plump or Craft. He demonstrated that in the '54 regional and semistate. He scored ten points against the host Lions in the Rushville Regional, then followed that with eight points in the victory over Aurora. The next weekend, Craft scored six points against Montezuma and topped those three efforts with thirteen points in the final with Attucks.

He recalls the final as his most complete game of that season. When Plump struggled, Craft kept the Indians in the lead early and then within striking distance. He had eleven points at halftime and finished with a game-high fourteen points, just under half his team's total points in the state championship game.

"As far as coming through when it needed to be done, it was in the championship game with the title on the line," Craft says.

That performance also turned the heads of those who would later vote for post-season awards and all-star teams. A few weeks after that game, Craft learned just how important others perceived his contribution to the team to be. He was selected to join Plump on the Indiana All-Star squad, making Milan the smallest school ever to put two players on the prestigious team.

Craft had enough talent for Tony Hinkle to enlist his services at Butler on a partial scholarship, but the majority of his playing days ended after that state tourney. "I really wasn't good enough to play for Butler," he says realistically. "I played very little basketball in college. As far as making an impact on a college team, there was only one who did that and that was Bob Plump."

By the time Craft got to college, basketball wasn't the top priority in his life. He was just glad to be there, getting an education at one of the top schools in Indiana. "It really gave me the opportunity to go to college," he said. "There was no way my parents could have afforded to send me to college."

He decided to major in education, but the coaching plans didn't really come into effect until later. It took an offhand recommendation from his college mentor to convince Craft that he could succeed in coaching. And the fact that he was a starting guard for that state champion four years earlier helped to open some doors in high school athletics.

"Hinkle told some people I should be a coach in an article," he said. "Name recognition might get somebody to notice you've applied. Then they're usually going to check up on you. It opened doors early for me. It's nice to have on your résumé because people can relate to it. People are more likely to consider you if they know something about you."

Craft's coaching career then took off. After graduating from Butler in 1958, he became the youngest high school coach in the state when he took over the program at Lapel.

His alma mater called after that one season, and Craft couldn't reject the offer. He lived at home and tried to resurrect the ghosts of Plump, White, Engel, Truitt, and himself. It wasn't an easy task. He did manage one sectional title, but that was a far cry from what he had accomplished as a player—two trips to the Final Four.

"We had some good ballclubs," Craft says. "I was confident or cocky enough to think that I was doing a good job. The realization came that everybody didn't think that. The pressure was there."

Craft ran into several roadblocks in his fourth year at Milan. The school board would not give him tenure. The superintendent, a good friend and one of his strongest supporters, died.

"I don't think they would have fired me," he says.

But he did know it was time to move on.

He traded his hometown roots for Clinton Central, where he coached five seasons and won a Frankfort Sectional title. He left the bench to move into an administrator's role as principal at Clinton Central for the next three years. He spent the following twelve years at Shelbyville, serving three as assistant principal and nine as principal.

That's when the IHSAA called, and Craft made the move to Indianapolis as an assistant commissioner. He's nearing ten years in that position and still lives in Shelbyville, an hour's drive from the IHSAA offices.

"I'm very happy I got this position and I enjoy it very much," he says. "Unless something drastic happens, I'll be here."

• • •

Now Craft is in a position of authority. He has gone from player to coach to administrator. He helps make the rules instead of just following them.

He will continue to be a main figure in any debate about breaking Indiana basketball into classifications. Football is the only IHSAA sport which currently has enrollment classes, with five different champions crowned each fall.

Craft must maintain a degree of impartiality in his role in the commissioner's office, but there's also no doubt that being a part of that Milan team will exert a strong influence.

"We do not have class basketball in Indiana for a couple of reasons," says Craft. "People don't like to be told they can't compete against the county seat. I don't think the fans are ready to give up one-class basketball. We talk to many other states that have class basketball, and they're amazed we can hold on to it. They say the longer you hold on to it, the better.

"People are never satisfied. If you have two classes, people will want three classes. There are schools that let it be known that they would like to see class basketball. There are groups out there that would like to see class basketball. I don't know if I'll ever see it or not, but I'm sure one day we'll see classes in basketball."

And while Craft grapples daily with problems that affect the state, he still receives personal achievement awards. Most of the people associated with the '54 Milan team were glad to see Craft get some deserved recognition in 1991 when he earned induction into the Indiana Basketball Hall of Fame. The team has a permanent display in the museum, but now Craft has joined Wood and Plump in the individual enshrinement hall. Many thought it was an honor that was long overdue.

"Being inducted into the Hall of Fame is the ultimate," says Craft. "It was a great honor for me just because of my background and athletics. I may not have been as concerned about it as some other people. We are all there as a team, and we earned our way there. I thought that maybe if I lived long enough and with my positions in athletics, I might have a shot at it."

In the next breath, Craft tries to turn the attention to someone else. In this case, it's the entire team.

He wants it on the record that the team won that title. Not Ray Craft. Not Bob Plump. Not Ron Truitt. The team.

"The thing I think is unfair is that in team games, individuals get the honors when it took the team to accomplish it," he says.

"Everyone played an important role on that team. I think Ray Craft has gotten more recognition than he could expect."

He might have been the sparkplug in an earlier day, but Craft now seems to be the one who will go quietly into the night. His place in the game is secure.

15 *Roger Schroder*

Roger Schroder still finds the 1954 Milan season an incredible tale. He coached high school basketball for twenty-two seasons, and he still can't believe that everything came together just right for the Indians all those years ago.

"I always felt like if you wrote the story, people would say that it can't be real," he says. "You just can't make it up to make it work out like that."

He says those words, breaks into a smile, and looks reflectively toward the ceiling. You get the feeling that he's trying to determine if it really did happen, if his Milan team really did beat Muncie Central for that state championship, the title that proved elusive as he chased it for twenty-two seasons as a head coach at Marshall and Broad Ripple, two schools in the Indianapolis Public School System.

Schroder started only one game in his two years on Milan's varsity team, but just being part of that championship effort means more to him than anything he could imagine.

"My life would be a lot different," Schroder says. "I don't

know what I could even think of to trade that for. Realistically, I wasn't that great a basketball player. The others deserved to play. I just made the contributions the best I could."

That championship eventually helped take Schroder to the capital city, a place that seemed so foreign to that group of boys who first played in the Indianapolis Semistate in 1953. He has coached in virtually every gym in Indianapolis, winning 218 total games, including three sectional championships.

Schroder's schedule for the 1990s is amazing. He teaches five math classes during the day at Broad Ripple, coaches the golf team each spring, and teaches night classes for almost four hours every Tuesday and Thursday. He gave up coaching the basketball team after the 1988 season when he realized something had to go.

When he does have time to relax, Schroder can do it in what amounts to his own solar system. He lives on the far east side of Indianapolis, in a secluded area near busy Interstate 70 that includes streets by the names of Astro, Constellation, Neptune, and Saturn.

"I guess," Schroder says, "they needed to come up with some new street names when they built the houses."

When he played at Milan and later at Franklin College, his future house was just a spot in a vast area of farmland. He, too, has seen the results of progress.

"I remember sitting with a guy over there," he says, pointing to a group of houses close to the main road. "He said, 'You know, the thing I like about living here is that there is all of this land and it is so quiet.' Now my house is right in the middle of where he was pointing."

He, like most of the other players on that team, is very modest about his achievement with Milan. He doesn't wear the championship ring, and he says he never brings the subject up in group conversation.

"I took off the ring when I went to college because I wanted to do whatever I could and not expect that to open some door for me because I was fortunate to be in the right place," he says. "I don't hide the fact, but I don't walk in and say, 'Hi, I'm Roger Schroder and I was on the state championship team.' It comes up, but not as much as it would if I pressed the issue."

• • •

Talk to Roger Schroder about his youth and the conversation almost always comes back to the store his grandfather started in 1904. He and his sister grew up in the first house across the railroad tracks in tiny Pierceville. The two-story house was flanked by the large general store that occupied most of his family's time and also put all of the meals on the table.

Carl and Helen Schroder opened the store at dawn and most often didn't close until dusk. It was strictly a family operation, one that took most waking hours to operate successfully.

"It was like the big discount stores now, like the Walmarts," recalls the youngest Schroder. "You could get anything from a can of soup to a television set. It was like the original mom and pop store. They worked from the moment they got up until the time they had to go to bed."

Schroder did his share of work at the store, but he also left plenty of time for sports. He became close friends with the other Pierceville kids, Bob Plump, Glenn Butte, Gene White, and future student manager Fred Busching. "We did what most young kids did—play basketball, play baseball, go swimming, go fishing," he says. "We had our chores we had to take care of, and when we could slip out, we would go out and play whatever was in season."

When he put that backboard in the alley behind the store, he became one of the most popular boys around. When he put that light up over the backboard and made night basketball possible, it was almost too good to be true.

"We liked to play more in the evening because it wasn't so hot," he says. "I rigged up a 300-watt light bulb, found an old piece of galvanized sheet metal, took a shovel, and hung that galvanized tin over it. I ran the extension cord out and the light just reflected over it. We played until time to go to bed."

Since most of the time was spent at the store, the Schroder family had very little time for vacations. They once went to the Wisconsin Dells, and sometimes they closed the store early on Saturdays to spend the night at a nearby campsite. Young Roger spent some time with his aunt and uncle upstate in Gary, where he would often fish on Lake Michigan.

During the school year, he participated in those lunchtime games that first pitted Pierceville against Milan before the younger boys united to play the older players.

Along with Plump, Schroder first decided to try out for the team in the seventh grade. "We just decided we would go out for basketball," he recalls. "We didn't know what we should play. We decided we should be forwards. We didn't know a forward from a whatever."

Schroder was one of a handful of players on that championship team who could have started for virtually every other school in Ripley County. But since there was so much talent among the five starters, especially the guards in Plump and Ray Craft, he had to settle for a role off the bench. After all, he was playing behind two Indiana All-Stars, two future members of the Indiana Basketball Hall of Fame. "Schroder was a smart ballplayer," says former assistant Marc Combs. "In my mind, he could have started on anybody's ballclub."

Schroder's role in both his junior and senior seasons became one of turning in quality minutes when Plump or Craft needed a breather. His only start was the game against Napoleon in 1953 when Marvin Wood suspended Plump for breaking the team curfew on New Year's Eve. He scored just two points in a 61–53 Milan victory, but he played a much larger role than that scoring figure indicated.

Scan the box scores from the 1954 season, and Schroder's name is not often listed. Wood used primarily a six-man rotation, and that left Schroder on the bench. He became one of the key practice players, the one who would guard Plump in simulating the defenses of opposing teams.

"Like any reserve player, you just had to be ready when you were called upon," he says. "You just had to work your butt off in practice. I always guarded Plump in practice. I couldn't stop him. But then a lot of guys couldn't guard him. He was too quick, and I wasn't even that slow. We used to play in the alley behind the store, and he was a little bigger and a little quicker and a little stronger. I wasn't physically able to beat him. He could take me one-on-one to the basket. He could get the ball off a little better because he was taller."

Schroder didn't play in any of the four games—the semistate or the state—at Butler Fieldhouse in 1954, but he was just as much a part of the team as Plump, White, or Craft. He knew that he had made as many sacrifices along the way for the success of that Milan team. Going into those final games, Schroder knew that he probably wouldn't play much, if at all. What he wasn't prepared for was the attention that he would receive for just being a part of the Indian squad.

Schroder's case is the perfect example of how much talent Milan actually had in 1954. While he played in few games as a senior that season, he received a partial scholarship to play basketball and baseball at Franklin College. When the deal was finalized, he had to pay just $640 a year for room and board plus the cost of his books.

He always thought he would attend college, but he had really never dreamed that he would still be able to play basketball. He had planned to enroll at Purdue and study engineering, to design the same type of television sets that his dad sold in the family store.

"I had applied and was accepted at Purdue," he says. "Then a solicitor came from Franklin College and asked if we [Schroder and Gene White] would be interested in going to Franklin. We went up there with him and it was fine. We met some real good people up there. I thought, 'Well, I could go to Purdue, do all of that, and watch the ballgames, or I could go to Franklin and maybe have a chance to play.' That's how I decided to go to Franklin, because of the opportunity to play."

At the same time, Schroder decided to switch from an engineering career to one in teaching and coaching. "I think it was a matter of being able to continue to compete," he says. "You don't have to give up the game. You can still continue to compete even though you're not on the floor."

He earned two varsity letters in basketball and three in baseball at Franklin. He would have been a four-year letter winner in baseball if not for a broken ankle that forced him to miss his sophomore season. He did play many more minutes on the basketball court at Franklin than he had at Milan, partly because, he admits, the team was not overly talented.

"The basketball at Franklin was just about the opposite of the basketball at Milan," Schroder says. "When I was a freshman, they had a good team and they won the conference. Then the seniors graduated, the coach left, and the players there just weren't good enough. I started some and played in most of the games. Nobody was outstanding. I've learned that when you don't have a player who is outstanding and everyone is about the

167

same, you're going to get beat. It was fun, but we didn't accomplish anything as far as championships."

When he graduated from college in 1958, Schroder had a variety of opportunities. He interviewed in Evansville and looked at coaching positions in Seymour, but the decision basically came down to three Indianapolis schools—Tech, Wood, and Howe. He found the best opportunity at Howe and became the coach of the freshman basketball and baseball squads. It was also in 1958 that he married his college sweetheart, Sue.

Schroder stayed at Howe for nine years, coaching the junior varsity basketball team for six seasons. The Indianapolis Public School System added brand-new John Marshall High School on East 38th Street in 1967, and Schroder became the head basketball coach there. He bought the house where he now lives and settled in for what would be a nineteen-year tenure. His first team at Marshall won seven games and lost fifteen, but the biggest factor was that the high school had no seniors during its first year of operation. So Schroder had his entire team back for the 1968–69 campaign. That team went an impressive 18–3 before losing 47–45 in the sectional to Shortridge, a team that advanced to the state finals that season.

"That second year was something," Schroder says. "Everybody was coming back, and everybody was so happy to have their own school. It was a brand-new school, totally air-conditioned. It was a beautiful school, kind of like a utopia. We even watched them put the floor down in the gym."

Schroder earned Marion County Coach of the Year honors after that second season, but the next few years would be marked by inconsistency. "We kind of had the doldrums after that," he says. "We had two years where the freshman team won one game each season. By the time they were seniors, we had to bite the bullet. Then we kind of swung back again."

Marshall did swing back, in impressive fashion. Schroder's team won the sectional in 1977, beat a Tech team with future Indiana standout Landon Turner in the semifinals of the 1978 city tournament, and won the sectional again in 1981 and 1983. Schroder coached two Indiana All-Stars: Larry Bullington, who played at Ball State and is now Connersville's head coach, and David "Poncho" Wright, who played on Louisville's 1980 NCAA champions—their championship coming at Market Square Arena in Poncho's hometown, Indianapolis.

But after that run of dominance, Marshall fell on hard times again. Enrollment dwindled, and the basketball program suffered. Schroder struggled to put together .500 seasons. Finally, the school system decided to close two high schools, and Marshall was one of the unlucky duo. The other was Crispus Attucks, Oscar Robertson's old school, closed with Marshall following the 1985–86 school year.

"They just closed her down," Schroder says. "You can still go over there now, and it's still one of the better-looking buildings in the city. It was just one of those political things. I didn't like that very well. I thought it was a raw deal. The people out there were blue-collar people. They didn't have anybody on the school board. Part of it was that Marshall was on the far east side, and if they were going to close a school [Attucks] which was historically black, then to appease some of the black people who thought it was wrong, they closed a school which was predominantly white. I think that was some of the social aspects of it.

"It was a darn good school. The last year we were open, we won the national award for excellence from the United States government. We're the only Indianapolis public school to get that. It's pretty hard to close down the only school to win that, but then again, it was all politics and social problems."

So after twenty-eight years as a teacher and coach, Schroder was without a job. The agreements of the closing specified that Schroder would automatically receive any head basketball coaching position which opened at any Indianapolis public school. The only problem was that no head coach left after the 1986 season.

That left Schroder in a predicament. He could either give up coaching entirely and take a teaching-only position, or he could become an assistant coach. He chose the assistant route again, this time at Manual High School. "I just thought I'd go down and enjoy the coaching and working with the kids," he said. "I also thought about teaching night school to earn a few extra bucks, so the next time they did something to me that I didn't like, I wouldn't necessarily have to put up with it."

In a strange twist of fate, Schroder stayed only three weeks at Manual. The head coaching position at Broad Ripple opened when Bill Smith resigned to take a post as the Center Township trustee. That meant Schroder would be the automatic choice to succeed Smith.

Two main problems resulted from this arrangement. First, many people within Broad Ripple had wanted the junior varsity coach to succeed Smith instead of Schroder. Second, Smith and Schroder were as different in life and coaching styles as night and day.

"There was a big difference," Schroder recalls about his transition as the head coach at Broad Ripple. "The coach who was at Broad Ripple had done things a whole lot differently. He was very successful, and he won the [1980] state championship. He did a lot of things to get kids to come to school there. He did things by intimidation. We saw things from a completely different perspective. They had wanted their assistant coach to move up. It was all cut and dried, and then here came this coach from Marshall and Manual. It was not easy."

Success was also not easy for Schroder at Broad Ripple. He was 40–25 in three seasons but could not win a sectional, the ultimate measure of a coach's value. In his final season, the Rockets beat North Central in the opening round of the tourney before losing to Lawrence North, a team that won the state title behind seven-foot center Eric Montross, who would later star at North Carolina.

Schroder finally decided that something had to go, and basketball became the casualty. He still teaches those five math classes, still coaches the golf team, and still conducts those marathon night sessions. But coaching the basketball team is no longer part of his daily routine. "I miss the competitive part," he says, "and some of the guys who were fun to coach against. I miss some of the good kids I had."

• • •

Schroder admits his life was once much simpler than it is in the nineties. He lives just two miles from the closed Marshall High School. He was the head coach there for nineteen seasons. People knew what to expect from him, and he knew what to expect from people.

The closing of Marshall and his eventual move to Broad Ripple changed that. Now he drives twenty-five miles to work instead of just two. He has progressed with the times, but it's easy to see that Schroder yearns for those simpler days.

His family has almost all moved on now. One daughter, Vicki, is an accountant in Indianapolis, and another daughter, Julie, is a first-grade teacher. His only son, Kent, is finishing his studies at Purdue and plans to become a teacher. Roger recently dug an old circus wagon out of the attic for his one-year-old granddaughter.

He has become more reflective over the years, about life in general and about Milan in particular.

"It was just too spectacular," he says. "How could anybody think about a little school like that getting to the finals once and then backing it up by winning it all the next year? It was just unbelievable. I realize more and more how fortunate we were and how things had to hit together just right."

Winning that title gave Schroder a new direction in life, but it also kept him wondering throughout his coaching years why he couldn't win that same state championship. "That was my dream, to win the state championship," he says. "It had been so great as a player, I think I would have enjoyed it more as an adult from the coaching standpoint. I just guess I wasn't a good enough coach. I didn't have what it took to get the right guys through at the right time."

But at least Schroder had that one dream back in 1954, the one that seemed more improbable than any other, the one that sent him to Franklin College, where he met his future wife, and to the high school coaching ranks, where he won 218 basketball games.

"I might have gone to Purdue, flunked out, and gone back to run my dad's store," he laughs. "I might have been an electrical engineer and maybe had a little bit fancier home. I had a math and physics comprehensive major. I should have gone into some industry and seen what there was, but I didn't do it. I guess I enjoyed what I was doing well enough to not go and check. I still enjoy what I'm doing, helping and seeing kids learn something."

Schroder plans to gradually cut back on his schedule and ease into retirement. "We'll just keep on keeping on," he says.

And when he finally does retire, there's always a little store in Pierceville that might be for sale.

16 *Bill Jordan*

Bill Jordan is the enigma from the 1954 Milan basketball team, the one who admits he never really fit in with everyone else.

Sure, he was part of the team. He's in every picture. His former teammates still mention him with a certain fondness. But there was something missing, something that kept Jordan from hanging on to the memory and the moment like Bob Plump or Bob Engel or Ray Craft.

Maybe it's because Jordan was just a junior in '54. Maybe it's because he didn't make the headlines like the other players. But probably it's because Jordan had a variety of interests that extended beyond the basketball court.

Almost everyone agrees on one thing about Bill Jordan: He could really play the piano.

He played before games, between games, after games. He was part of a band that performed at weekend dances.

Jordan was the musical talent on the athletic basketball team. His teammates often gathered around him as a way to relax and ease the pressures of the long seasons. His talents eventually landed Jordan in Hollywood, where he has spent a career in movies, television, and commercials.

But along the way, there came a tradeoff. Jordan rarely returns to his hometown, rarely sees his former teammates. Ray Craft last saw Jordan when they had breakfast thirty years ago in California. Ken Wendelman can't remember talking with Jordan since he graduated from high school.

"Bill was always his own man," says Wendelman, who also fits in that category.

One senses a certain uneasiness when Jordan thinks back to the Milan days. He stresses over and over that he doesn't want to take a thing away from that championship run. He thought it was amazing then. He thinks it's amazing now.

The difficulty comes when he tries to determine his place in that history, how it affected him then and how it affects him all these years later.

"I still feel a little uncomfortable about it," Jordan says. "I kind of felt left out. I was certainly a cheerleader for it. Those guys were a wonderful group of guys. But I never felt like one of them, even though I was on the team and contributed. I felt alienated from the rest.

"I never looked back. I'm really proud of it. I still have the ring in a safe-deposit box. I don't want to take anything away from it. It was a great accomplishment. It's just like a dream that I don't know how to celebrate. It's just a memory."

• • •

Bill Jordan lived an average childhood in Milan like most of the other players on the team. "I never wanted for anything but I worked for what I got," he says. "I didn't have to worry about a clean place to sleep or having food on the table."

What he did worry about came as a result of his musical interest and ability. Jordan had taken lessons since an early age, and that didn't win him many popularity contests in a town driven by basketball, baseball, and more basketball.

"I had always taken lessons and that was unheard of," says Jordan. "My mother pushed me toward that. I always played in the high school band. A lot of times there was a matter of priorities—basketball or the band. Obviously, basketball was more important at the time.

"I remember a few people—and I don't even know who they are now—always reminded me I was in the band. It was almost insinuating that I was a sissy. It never really stopped me. If there was a play or a band concert, I was there. It didn't affect me a lot. I had to somehow become bigger than all of that. I must say though that sports was my main thought. I was able to have an immediate gratification from it."

Before he could go to Hollywood—and that wasn't really a goal for him in high school—Jordan first concentrated on a high school sports career.

He was an underclassman, along with Rollin Cutter and Glenn Butte, on that '54 championship team. As a sophomore he had played on the junior varsity in Milan's first Final Four season. During the championship season he played an important role off the bench as one backup for Plump and Craft and scored a game-high fifteen points in the sectional opener, an 83–36 victory over Cross Plains.

He received spot play the remainder of the season and came back to great expectations in his senior season. He helped the Indians win the sectional in his senior year, the top guard and the team leader. But those teams could never come close to the glory of the previous seasons. No matter how much individual success Jordan had later, in Milan he was remembered primarily as a junior member of the only team that mattered.

After high school, Jordan attended Indiana University on an ROTC scholarship and then the University of Vienna—with a brief tryout and stint in the Cincinnati Reds baseball organization sandwiched in between. Even though he had immense experience in music, he decided to pursue a career in acting. "Being a musician was not the lifestyle I wanted," he says. "There was a great deal of uncertainty—the night life, being on the road." He earned a spot in the 20th Century Fox talent pool in Hollywood, but that quickly ended when the air force called him to duty in Korea and Japan.

After one year overseas, he was based in New York City, where he produced the air force radio show "Country Music Time." He often made trips to Nashville to interview such artists as Tex Ritter, Roy Clark, and Dolly Parton. After his military stint, Jordan remained in New York to begin—for the second time—his acting career. On Broadway, he made good impressions—and received critically acclaimed reviews—for his work as the young professor in *Who's Afraid of Virginia Woolf* with Shelley Winters, and as George C. Scott's son Richard in *The Lion in Winter.* He was in *Wait until Dark* with Lee Remick.

"Those first jobs in New York City were enormous breaks," he says. "The first jobs are like a vote of confidence."

He received many more votes of confidence as he began to commute between New York and Hollywood for numerous television series—"Rat Patrol," "Bonanza," and "High Chaparral." The work in New York's theater still excited him, and that kept him based in the Big Apple rather than in Hollywood. "The longer you can stay away the better you are," he says of Hollywood. "Once you're in California, you're in an industry rather than an art form."

In all, Jordan has appeared in more than fifty television shows, playing the full scope of characters from former president John F. Kennedy to notorious outlaw John Dillinger. He even hosted "Project UFO" for several seasons before "philosophy conflicts" convinced him to pursue other projects. He says now, "If I had stuck with that show for two or three more years, I would be a much richer man."

Jordan's movie credentials are also impressive. His eight full-length films include *Rage, Truman Capote Trilogy, A Man Called Horse,* and *Nothing but a Man.* In *The Buddy Holly Story,* the man with a music background learned the significance of rock and roll.

"I was never a rock-and-roll musician," he says. "I always put it down. Then I got to be in one of the better stories of a rock-and-roll musician there ever was. *The Buddy Holly Story* was just an honest-to-goodness story about a kid who grew up in Lubbock, Texas. There were a lot of good things about rock and roll that I never appreciated. I thought it was an awful veering off course for music. I was into the standards. How much I was proven wrong."

Jordan admits it is much tougher to break into Hollywood today. A potential star must have the right mix of talent, luck, and timing. He was fortunate to have all three, but he also realizes everything could change tomorrow.

"Even now, I'm not a star," he says. "I'm just a working actor. I've made a living at it for twenty-five years. This is fleeting. You're only as good as your last credit."

• • •

Jordan says he doesn't miss Milan and the Midwest. He also knows many of those values remain inherent even though almost four decades have elapsed since he graduated from high school in 1956. "I don't think I've lost a lot of that," he says. "There's still a lot of the Midwest in me. I think it's a real honest part of Americana."

And perhaps the Midwest helped shape Jordan's view—and also contributed to his success—in Hollywood. He may not consider himself a star, but he has made a comfortable living over the years. He's appeared alongside many of the biggest names in Hollywood, and the fact that producers keep asking him back speaks louder than any other tribute. In his mid-fifties now, Jordan says the lure of the big screen is gone, that the changes have taken their toll on him over the past three decades.

"I've been more money-oriented since I came out here," he says. "I do it because it's my job and to make a living. Now I'm more interested in the quality of life than in the acting profession."

Jordan has been a survivor in what has developed into a business where the odds of success become thinner with each wave of new talent. His credits fill an entire page, and he's not finished yet. In fact, he thinks the finale may never come.

"I have not realized my potential," he says. "But a lot of us in life don't. I had to make some compromises to make sure I could make a living."

And if he had it to do all over again, would Jordan still insist on going against the current? Would he still insist on the fine arts, or would he trade the jeers for cheers solely on the basketball court?

"I think I would be an opera singer," he says.

17 *Glenn Butte*

It's the middle of a warm spring day, and Glenn Butte is having some work done on his automobile at the Milan General Motors dealership. He lives about fifteen minutes north in Batesville, but still buys his cars in his hometown of Milan, probably out of loyalty more than anything else.

Butte was one of the biggest members of that championship team at 6-5, and he is still a commanding presence. But the attention he commands in Milan is never because of his size, but because he was a sophomore member of that '54 Indian squad.

People still recognize him in Milan solely because of his feats on the basketball court.

"It's nice to be recognized here," he says. "I sit here and people walk through and say 'Hi,' and I have no idea who they are. They recognize me, and I've been away from here thirty years. Any member of our championship team is still a hero in this town, maybe this county."

Butte has also remained close to Milan, both in distance and in heart. He didn't design it that way. It just kind of happened.

He, Rollin Cutter, and Bill Jordan were the three underclassmen on that championship team. Butte had to endure two more seasons of the legacy he helped to create. He was a star in his junior and senior seasons, earned a scholarship at Indiana, and coached at several schools before ending up at Batesville High School, about twenty miles north of Milan.

Butte has seen just about everything in his more than thirty-five years associated with high school athletics. He's seen more sectional and county tournaments and state finals than he can remember. They all run together after a while. He is a fount of basketball knowledge.

No one really cares about that, though. Everyone wants to talk about the '54 season, the one where he played a reserve role as Milan dreamed all the way to a state title. He didn't really know what it meant then. He still struggles with what it means today.

"As a fifteen-year-old sophomore on a state championship team, I had no idea what we had accomplished," says Butte. "I knew we had won the state championship. I knew we were the champions of Indiana. I knew it was great. The next morning in the papers, I began to realize a little bit what had happened. The longer it goes, the more I appreciate the talent and the luck that goes into winning a state championship."

Butte still wears that championship ring he earned many seasons ago. He still talks in disbelief about the Indians beating the Bearcats in Butler Fieldhouse.

A lot has happened in Butte's life since 1954, but, as with so many of his teammates, everything goes back to the past. No matter what will happen, nothing can change what has already happened.

Once a hero, always a hero.

"When we were seventh- and eighth-graders, we were happy to win the Ripley County championships," says Butte. "We thought that was the greatest thing that had happened in Milan in years. Milan had never won a game in the regional. Then to win the regional, that was unheard of. There was no way we could have known, no way we could have judged. . . . "

• • •

Glenn Butte grew up as one of the Pierceville farm boys. His family owned fifty acres of land, a holding that has since grown to more than five hundred acres. His father, Charles, also operated a trucking, sand, and gravel business. In an area where people had very little, the Butte family enjoyed an above-average economic situation.

"We had a comfortable life as far as living where we did," says Butte. "We had trucks and tractors because we were farmers. We were also able to buy our first new car at the end of World War II. That was quite a fashionable status symbol. They weren't available even if you had the money. We had a television and spent a lot of time watching wrestling and westerns.

"A visit to Milan once a week was probably the highlight. Milan had a movie theater then, and I rode in with Bob Plump's dad, who usually went to the lodge meetings. I'd just go to the movies and then come home later with him."

Butte says his parents have never taken a vacation, and he hadn't been to Indianapolis until the '53 semistate. About the only big city he had ever visited was nearby Cincinnati when he was a youngster, and that was a trip he would like to forget.

"As a kid, I played baseball a lot," he says. "We went to Cincinnati for a game, and I got a nosebleed after the game. I tried to keep up with the crowd, got lost, tried to find the bus, and couldn't find it. A police officer saw me, and he got me calmed down enough to ask me where I was from. The bus had left and was headed back toward Milan. Fifteen miles outside of Cincinnati, the police turned the siren on the bus and I got back on."

Butte didn't make many more trips outside of Ripley County in his youth. One scare was enough. He was happy to stay in Pierceville with Plump, Schroder, and White. Even though they were two years older than he, Butte still found himself in their company most of the time.

But when he was younger, baseball was the real game of choice. He liked basketball, but he doesn't remember ever dreaming about playing on the high school team. He began playing at Plump's old goal in about the fourth grade and finally saw his first high school game two years later.

"From that day on, there was not a day that went by, 365 days a year, that someone was not playing basketball," he says.

His encouragement to play came from an unlikely source—his mother. In fact, his father never saw him play a game in his three seasons on the varsity. Mildred Butte, once a softball pitcher in local leagues and a member of the girls' basketball team in her high school days, served as her son's inspiration.

Butte made the traditional climb through the ranks, playing on the grade school teams under Marc Combs and then on the junior varsity as a freshman. Butte was the workhorse on a junior varsity team that was loaded with so much talent that it probably would have defeated many varsity teams in the area.

There was one time in particular that Butte found out just how much of that talent was expendable.

"I had twenty-four points at the end of the third quarter," he recalls. "The coach took me out and said he wanted me to go down to the varsity dressing room. I thought I was going to get to play with the varsity that night. It turned out one of the varsity players had misplaced his jersey, and he wanted to use mine. He said I could just go ahead and take a shower."

Coach Marvin Wood did ask Butte to practice with the team during the tournament, although IHSAA rules prevented him from sitting on the bench. So he rode with Roger Schroder's dad to the games and became a fan instead of a player.

"I was 100 percent for them," he says. "I really didn't feel like I needed to be on the team then. I was just a true fan."

The next year was a different story. He earned what he thought was a well-deserved spot on the varsity. "I would have been very disappointed if I had not made it," he says. "I was one of the tallest players on the team, and I thought my offense was good enough. I got to start a few games and played a lot as a substitute."

It was as a substitute that he made his biggest contribution to that team. Milan was playing Versailles in the sectional and not having the expected easy time. Two factors complicated this game—it was being played on Versailles' home court, and it was the fourth meeting of the season between the two teams. With each game, it became tougher and tougher for the Indians to defeat their old rivals.

Milan clung to just a one-point lead, 28–27, midway through the third quarter. That's when Wood inserted Butte into the lineup.

"I think Woody, in a little bit of desperation, put me in the game to play a little tighter defense," says Butte.

What Wood didn't expect was for Butte to explode on the other end of the court. With Milan holding that slim advantage and Versailles looking for the upset, Butte scored the game's next eight points to give the Indians some breathing room and an eventual victory.

"I feel like my contribution to the championship season was to help them get out of the sectional," he says. "It was hard to beat a team for the fourth time, particularly a good ballclub. And they were a good ballclub."

Butte played spot roles in the remaining tourney games, including the state championship contest with Muncie Central. But when it was over, he was one of the three who stayed behind. Still, he wasn't upset that he didn't go out in a blaze of glory like the seven seniors. "If I had been a senior, I might have screwed things up," he says. "We might not have won the championship."

Butte, Cutter, and Jordan would receive a lot more playing time in the next two seasons, but there would also be the constant pressure to live up to lofty expectations. It was a pressure that was there, but something that Butte never thought about or feared on a regular basis.

"I knew I would play a bigger role," he says. "I didn't feel any pressure. We were oblivious to pressure. I don't think we knew what it was. I had no idea what winning the state championship meant. I wanted to come back and do it again. There was no idea what skill and luck you had to have to do it. I knew we didn't have a Plump. I knew we didn't have a Craft. We did have some good size."

Milan won its first five games in the fall of '54, then once again won the county tournament and the sectional. In the sectional, Butte again victimized Versailles. The game was tied after one overtime, and the rules then called for sudden death, where the first team to score two points was the winner. Butte rebounded a missed shot and put it in to give the Indians their third straight sectional championship. The run of tournament championships ended in the regional; Milan lost to Rushville in the evening championship contest.

The next season, Butte's last, was almost identical. Milan won its fifth consecutive county tournament, its fourth straight sectional, and lost again in the regional final, this time to Connersville. Butte ended his high school career in grand fashion, scoring twenty-eight points while missing just one field goal against the Spartans.

Butte's career ended with three county tournament titles, three sectionals, a regional, a semistate, and a state championship. But the last two years, while they were successful, left the spoiled fans wanting a little more because of the success Milan had had in '54.

"They were disappointed we didn't win the state my junior and senior years," says Butte. "However, we had gone farther than any team except the '53 and '54 teams. People were upset because they had been to the Final Four the past two seasons."

Butte thinks that performance in a losing cause against Connersville got him his full scholarship to Indiana University under legendary Hoosier coach Branch McCracken. Connersville coach Ken Gunning had played at Indiana in the late thirties and passed the word to McCracken about Butte's ability.

"I'm sure that was the turning point," says Butte. "That was probably the best game of my career. I probably never would have attended college, and I don't know what I would have been doing today—maybe farming or working in a factory somewhere. That opened the door for me."

Butte spent the next four years at Indiana, earning a varsity letter in his senior season in 1960. Like five other members of that '54 team, he majored in education and wanted to become a coach. The only problem was that those jobs were scarce when he graduated in the spring of 1960.

He eventually took a position at Moore's Hill, the school that had hired Herman Grinstead when he left Milan in '53. Butte became Grinstead's assistant and served as the head coach of the baseball team. He stayed two years at Moore's Hill, now part of South Dearborn High, and then left for Dillsboro. He spent five years there, one as assistant basketball coach and four as the head man.

The third stop for Butte came at Orleans High School. That stay was brief, just one season, before he and his wife learned that her father had cancer. They wanted to be near his Milan hometown, and Butte applied for a job at nearby Batesville. That's where he's been for more than two decades now, first as a combination assistant principal and athletic director and now solely as athletic director.

He hopes that he has made his mark, that people will remember him for his influence and his contributions.

"I want them to remember I was part of the championship team, a person who through my living has been a good example for youth. I've been able to stay with youth through athletics and promote athletics as a fine avenue for young men and women to participate in."

• • •

Back at Batesville High School, Butte gives the impression of a man content with his job and surroundings. He oversees a program that is good, but by no means on the edge of greatness. The Bulldogs, who have won just one regional in their history, are a consistent .500 team.

Unless something drastic happens, Butte plans to hang it up at Batesville in a few years, just a few miles up the road from his old hometown of Milan. He will leave content, accomplishing just about what he wanted.

But at the same time Butte has been making his contribution at Batesville, he has watched the Milan basketball program die a slow death. It's been a long, downhill ride from the success Butte's teams enjoyed.

"When you win, you get a little spoiled with success," says Butte. "The people in Milan, the four years I was in high school, we had four county championships, four sectionals, two Final Fours. It was over twenty years until they won another sectional.

"I would like to see the basketball team get a winning record and be competitive again," he says. "It's sad to see. But it's no one's fault, not the coach, not the school."

Butte would be more likely to put the blame on the system in general, where kids just don't have the dedication and desire to become state champion.

"I think the biggest thing that I see now is the automobile," says Butte. "We have an enrollment of 500 students at Batesville. I can take you out to the parking lots and there would be 250–300 automobiles. The automobile is so much more important than winning the varsity letter is today.

"What has happened is that mom and dad have given in and said you can drive the automobile. Then, mom and dad tell them they have to put the gas in, pay the insurance, make the payments. So then they have to work. Out of 500 kids here, about 150 work at least fifteen hours a week to pay for automobiles. If they're working that many hours a week, they can't participate in any extracurricular activities. The automobile and the part-time job have played the biggest part in why the kids aren't in the gyms on Friday and Saturday nights.''

It's definitely not like it was in the fifties, when basketball was king. Butte knows times change. He just goes on and tries to adjust.

''We didn't have any other entertainment,'' he says. ''We didn't have our own cars. We didn't go tooling around like they do today. Basketball became an obsession with us because it was an outlet to do something. Without basketball, I don't know what we would have done.''

For one thing, they wouldn't have won a state championship. And Butte would probably be riding a tractor on that 500-acre farm in Pierceville.

''Things have worked out for me,'' says Butte.

18 *Rollin Cutter*

A few years ago, Rollin Cutter took a short drive from his Noblesville home to the Indiana Basketball Hall of Fame, then located in Indianapolis. His son, Rob, eighteen at the time, had never seen the tape of the 1954 state championship between his dad's team and Muncie Central.

Rob took a friend and rode thirty minutes to finally see what all these people had been talking about all these years. He had heard the stories grow larger and larger each year. Now he wanted to see the real thing.

"On the way down," says the elder Cutter, "I said, 'I want you to promise me that you won't laugh when you see the tape.' We drove down there and they laughed. They started chuckling right when they saw the six-foot free-throw lanes and the fact that the jump shot was just coming into existence. You see Ron Truitt fire up a floating one-hander. You see Gene Flowers putting up a twenty-five- or thirty-foot shot from the sidelines. The game was played so differently than it is today. It's hard for people to understand how different it was. It's hard to understand how you could just stand there and hold the ball."

Cutter was one of the youngsters on the team, one of just two sophomores who took part in the '54 state finals for Milan. And he wasn't on the team solely because he made a good practice player. He was a contributor, playing in the shadows of Plump, Craft, Truitt, et al.

He had a role, and he knew what it was. He also knew that his big days would come in the next two seasons as a junior and senior. For now, it was a learning experience, a time to fit in when needed. "Woody played me as much as he could," says Cutter. "I didn't look back and feel that I didn't get my playing time. I got to play probably as much as I would have under any other circumstances."

It was in the finals that Cutter made the biggest impact on the basketball floor, and he knows just being a part of that team opened doors that probably would have remained closed.

"I appreciate the opportunity I had, the ideals, the way I grew up," he says. "I would never have gone to college had it not been for basketball."

But Cutter did go to college, graduated, and then spent a lifetime in high school sports. He hung the whistle up for good a few years ago, but he remains guidance director at Noblesville High School, a couple of hours north of Milan. It's an upscale, growing community, one with a number of contrasts to his hometown of Milan.

But don't get the idea that he and his wife, Maridee, also a Milan graduate, necessarily like it better than the hometown. It's just a different generation, a different time. There was a time to move on. There is now a time to stay put.

Cutter talks easily and at length about his childhood days in Milan. He has an appreciation for the kind of person that town made him. He will always be a legend in the town, but he might be nothing without it.

"I knew the town as some very, very good people, some very friendly people," says Cutter. "Everybody knew you and where you lived. People would go out of their way to help you. If anything, I would miss the town more if that wasn't true today. People know each other. People help each other. I still have fond memories of the whole place."

He knows who gave him his beginning. Cutter, like the rest of the players on that '54 team, hasn't forgotten his roots.

• • •

Rollin Cutter was one of the farm boys on the championship team. His parents owned a 150-acre farm about five miles northwest of Milan, and he spent most of his early youth working in those fields. He and his two brothers had a variety of chores on the farm that served as home for cattle, pigs, and chickens. In the summers, they would rise before dawn and not finish work until long after the sun had set. "We were all expected to help on the farm," Cutter says. "I can remember from when I was five or six years old doing work that today you wouldn't expect kids to do."

On the surface and by the standards of the nineties, it doesn't sound like a desirable life. By the standards of the fifties, it was considered normal.

"We didn't want for anything," says Cutter. "I would say we were very typical of other small farmers in the area. If you compare with what people have today, we didn't have much. I can never think that we needed anything as far as money or worldly needs. We would work all week and then go to town on Saturday night.

"We always went to church on Sunday morning. Sunday, back then, was a dedicated rest day. You didn't work on Sunday. That's not true today. Even if it rained all week and Sunday was the best day we had, we would deliberately not work on Sunday."

Basketball wasn't on the list of Cutter's daily chores, but he did find time to play. Some neighbors introduced him to the game when he neared grade-school age, and he often played at the goal in a barn owned by his uncle. When his uncle, who was ten years older, graduated from high school, Cutter convinced his grandfather to hang the goal at the family farm. It still hangs in the barn today, and Cutter's father still owns the land.

"I was interested in basketball as early as I can remember," he says. "That was back in the second and third grade."

The basketball bug really bit Cutter as he progressed through grade school. He remembers playing against the older kids—he was two years younger than the senior class of '54—during every recess. He also spent most Sundays playing with the neighbors. A spot on the junior high team seemed inevitable in the sixth grade, so he asked his father's permission to try out for the squad.

"I remember asking my dad if I could play basketball," says Cutter. "He said, 'I guess you can, but I can't come get you after practice.' So I went out as a sixth-grader and walked home."

The Cutter farm was more than five miles from the Milan school.

"That's what I wanted to do, and I didn't mind walking home," he says. "My older brother didn't play because he didn't want to walk home. Ray Craft and I would usually hitchhike or just walk home after practice. It was fifteen minutes from his house to my house. I didn't mind it at all. If it was raining, we might get a ride. My kids today don't want to hear that story. They laugh at me. There weren't too many things going on. I was in the eighth grade before we got our first TV. There wasn't any other entertainment.

"I was still expected to do things on the farm when I got home. I can remember many nights coming home from basketball and before I could sit down and have something to eat, I would go out and shovel a load of corn or something. It was part of my job and part of my responsibility. I didn't feel like I was being deprived or being picked on. It was just something that I was expected to do. I accepted it with no questions."

Cutter says that junior high coach Marc Combs found a place for him to play in the sixth grade. After that, Cutter had established himself as a bona fide player. He was good enough to play on the junior varsity during his freshman season in '53 and even practiced with the varsity through the state tournament.

Since rules limited teams to just ten players on the bench, Cutter watched from the stands as Milan raced through the sectional, regional, and semistate before losing to South Bend Central at the state. He had a cousin who lived in Indianapolis and stayed for the finals that night. That's when the importance of the tourney really hit home.

"That was the first time I had ever really sat in the stands and watched," he says. "I remember a great deal of disappointment that we lost, and I thought we lost pretty badly.

"I had been to Indianapolis for the state fair once or twice. If we went to the city, it was always Cincinnati. Any news we got came from Cincinnati. We knew very little about state tournaments and state championships. At least, I didn't know very much. In '53, it was my first experience as to what a state tournament was all about. I didn't realize until I had seen the night game how important it really was. We stayed over that night and saw the newspapers and the TV and saw how much importance it was given. Then it became a goal."

Before it could become a personal goal, however, Cutter had to make the varsity team. It looked like he had a chance, since Jim Wendelman and Jim Call had graduated, but there was stiff competition. Glenn Butte and Bob Wichman had both talent and potential. Cutter went through the tryouts and then hoped for the best.

"I think I was probably as surprised as anybody that I made the team," says Cutter. "Someone else told me my name was on the list. I went down, checked it for myself, and it was on the list. I was real pleased."

After he made the team, Cutter realized the toughest task would be convincing the coaching staff that he was good enough to actually play in some games. He didn't want to become a permanent fixture on the bench, but he also knew the starters were all tough and experienced.

His big opportunity came when Engel suffered the back injury early in the season. The bulk of the responsibility would fall on three players—Cutter, Butte, and Wendelman. Cutter's first start came against Napoleon in one of only two games played the entire season in Milan's home gymnasium. He responded with a solid effort. "I remember how nervous I was until I touched the ball," he says. "Then it seemed everything was back to natural."

Cutter spelled Engel on several occasions during the regular season, but Engel seemed fit as the tournament began. Engel exploded in the regional against Aurora and played consistently in the two semistate games. It seemed that Cutter would ride out the rest of his sophomore season on the bench.

But Engel's back injury worsened at each step of the tournament. He knew he would start each game, but anything after the first few minutes was doubtful. That meant Cutter would probably have a significant role to play in the state finals. Cutter didn't know it. He had no idea of the seriousness of Engel's injury.

"Early in the week, I stayed after practice a couple of times working with Woody and the assistant coach on offense," says Cutter. "I didn't associate that with anything that was forthcoming. I didn't know how bad Bob was hurt. He didn't practice very hard. [But] Woody didn't say anything and I didn't ask. Even before the game, he didn't say to be ready or tell me what was going to happen."

Midway through the first quarter of the afternoon game with Terre Haute Gerstmeyer, Wood motioned for Cutter to sit next to him on the Milan bench. Cutter entered the game at the end of the quarter. He hit a field goal and a free throw for three points, and his presence up front helped offset Gerstmeyer's inside game.

Cutter had just as big a role in the evening game. Although he didn't score a point, he played more than twenty minutes of consistent basketball. He replaced Engel midway through the first period and played until being lifted for Ken Wendelman with about two minutes left in the game. He confesses that he didn't even see Plump's last-second shot because someone jumped in front of him, but he knew from the sound of the crowd what had happened.

He may not have scored a point, but he had been the pre-game star. As he ran onto the court for warmups, the crowd had serenaded him with an offbeat version of "Happy Birthday." He turned sixteen the day Milan won the state championship.

During his senior season—disrupted in December because of a back injury—Cutter began to receive inquiries from several colleges. Tony Hinkle wanted him to join Plump and Craft at Butler. Franklin College wanted him to join White and Schroder. He also took a long look at and a visit to Louisville. He chose Butler, partly because of Hinkle and partly because of his former teammates, and became the first person in the Cutter family to embark on a college degree.

His collegiate career turned out to be plagued by injuries. He was a member of the Butler freshman team in '56 when he hurt his knee just before the Christmas break, and his career suffered a serious setback. "I turned nineteen, lived in a fraternity, and gained about thirty pounds by the end of the year," he says. He jokes that those extra thirty pounds are still with him today.

Cutter played some during his sophomore year, but didn't have the stamina and drive because of the knee injury. After hobbling through his junior season, he decided to give up playing the game and to concentrate on coaching it. He married Maridee, his high school sweetheart, before his senior year in college (they had their first date two days after the '54 state finals) and began to search for teaching and coaching positions.

He graduated from Butler in 1960 and became one of the youngest basketball coaches in the state when he took the head job at Syracuse High School in northern Indiana. He stayed there four years, compiled what he calls "about a 50-50" winning record, and moved on to Brownsburg. He coached there for two seasons, then became an administrator, the school's athletic director.

As Marvin Wood did when he went to Shelbyville, Cutter quickly learned that he missed coaching. He also knew that with a wife and two kids he needed some sort of stability. As a result, he entered the Indianapolis Public School System as an assistant coach at Arlington. He served in that capacity for seven years before leaving coaching for good. He went to Carmel High School as a counselor in 1974, then to neighboring Noblesville as the guidance director just five years later. He served a short stint as principal of Noblesville's junior high school, then returned to the high school as guidance director.

Cutter has lived in Noblesville since '72, when he still worked at Arlington. He plans to be there for a while longer. The kids are gone—daughter Marcia is twenty-nine and lives in Columbus, Ohio, and son Rob is the head football coach at Franklin Central High School.

It's back like the old days now. It's just Cutter and his wife, the two Milan graduates. This time, there are no impending plans.

"I plan on staying where I am," Cutter says. "The Good Lord willing and if the creek don't rise, I'll be here doing what I'm doing."

• • •

Perhaps Cutter more than anybody realizes how different the game is today. One of the three players who weren't seniors on that '54 team, he endured the legacy that he helped to create. He coached for thirteen seasons in Indiana; he saw the legacy grow.

He followed the same path as seven of the ten players on that championship squad. He went to college in Indiana, received his degree in physical education, and then became a coach.

He sees no irony in the fact that everyone associated with that team has since moved on to bigger things. It's just the way the world works, he says. Milan opened doors that probably would have remained shut.

In the end, everything comes back to his hometown. Milan didn't change Cutter. It defined him.

"There were two influences I had," he says. "My mother encouraged me to do well academically and to take courses that would prepare me for college. Marvin Wood influenced me from the standpoint of coaching and education. I think he did more on not just being a coach but being the type of person and leader he was. He led by example."

Cutter misses the small town, where you never passed a strange face. He lived in Indianapolis for several years and never got a feel for it the way he had in Milan. The people weren't as friendly. No one helped the neighbors.

He knows also that he will never return to Milan. He had the chance in the early seventies when the school board offered him the job as head basketball coach. He rejected it, partly because he was settled with his family, and partly because he was the second choice.

Too much has changed in the past thirty-five years since he graduated in '56. For one thing, kids don't walk five miles to get home after practice. Most drive home in their own vehicles. In a lot of instances, they don't even want to play.

"Basketball was fun for us," he says. "Going to practice was fun. In the summer when I was working, we would have an hour off for lunch. We would grab a sandwich and play basketball for fifty minutes. Kids don't do that today. They feel like they're expected to be in the gym all the time. One of the reasons I got out of coaching was because of the demands on the coach, to open up the gym, to have a weight program, to have a running program, to play basketball twelve months a year.

"I don't feel kids need to dedicate themselves that much. I think they need the opportunity to experience other things. They don't look forward to practice now. I never regretted a single practice. I thought it was fun. We had a good time. I don't think kids look at it like that today. There wasn't the individual competition that there is now."

Cutter seems glad that he was a kid in the fifties rather than the nineties. He wouldn't trade the experience for anything.

"We were pretty simple people," he says. "We weren't very sophisticated. We worked hard. We enjoyed it. The values my parents tried to teach me of hard work, of what things are worth, were almost ideal for the experiences I've had since then. I think it was an excellent beginning."

The rest of the trip hasn't been so bad either.

19 *Conclusion*

The small high school is on the endangered species list in Indiana. Consolidations have made it a recollection rather than a reality. In many cases during the late fifties and sixties, anywhere from two to four schools, sometimes as many as ten, merged to form one larger school. Milan survived, but many of the other small schools from that era became extinct. Only the old scorecards remain.

That change has meant two things to the Milan saga. First, it makes it far more unlikely that any small school could actually win the state championship in the nineties. Not only are there fewer small-school teams, but the quality of the bigger teams has also increased with the consolidation and addition of other schools. Inevitably, each year, as big schools take home the title, more proponents line up for either a tourney based on classes or one entirely for the small schools.

Neither of those second changes will happen, at least in the foreseeable future. The influential figures in Indiana high school sports are middle-aged men who well remember the miracle of

Milan. Maybe even more than that, most of the ten players from that '54 team still hold important positions—whether as administrators or as outside voices—within the IHSAA. Ray Craft is an assistant commissioner for the entire state.

It's true that no small school has won the state championship since Milan accomplished the feat in '54, and only a few have made a legitimate run for the title. Argos, a small school in north-central Indiana, advanced to the Final Four in 1979 before losing in the afternoon game. L & M, in southern Indiana, reached the Final Eight in 1986 and was featured in *Sports Illustrated* and *Esquire* (the latter in an on-the-spot piece done by renowned author David Halberstam).

But the *possibility* still exists for one of those teams to capture the hearts of a state and the title. It's that remote chance that has kept Indiana as one of only three states—Kentucky and Delaware being the others—where all teams play for one basketball championship.

The IHSAA did convert the annual football tournament into five classes more than a decade ago, but the basketball showcase has remained intact. And the fans still attend in record numbers. More than 41,000 people watched Damon Bailey lead his Bedford North Lawrence team to the '90 crown in the Hoosier Dome, the same building where 67,000 fans watched a summer exhibition game between the Olympic team and a group of NBA all-stars in 1984 and where 41,000 saw Duke win the 1991 NCAA Championship.

"A lot of people thought when we went to classes in football that would be the first step," says IHSAA public relations director Bob Williams, whose office is adjacent to Craft's. "Football is much different. We were interested in setting up a structure where everyone could enter the tournament. Football is a different sport, a physical sport."

Everyone connected with that '54 team has an opinion on class basketball. The coach and the players think their victory ensured the continued one-class tournament. They are probably right, although it is still unknown whether that one season can keep the tourney unchanged.

What many underestimate is the long-term satisfaction a small-school player gets from beating the big-name schools in the sectional or regional.

195

"I like the style of tournament we have," says Marvin Wood. "I attended a small high school in Morristown, and we won the sectional. It was like winning the state title to us. If we had never been in the tournament, we would never have had the opportunity. I think the small school deserves a chance. I think it would hurt a lot more than people realize. We would have more champions, but I don't think we would have the overall interest in the tournament.

"If a small school gets an exceptional player or two players and a good supporting cast, I think they can get the job done. They have to have some size, get a good tournament draw, and the ball has to bounce their way. I am convinced another small school will win it someday."

Says Glenn Butte, "I think it will stay the same for several years. When we won the championship in '54, there were some 700-odd teams. Now we have some 300-odd teams. We've lost a lot of the schools to consolidation. Most of the schools now are closer together in size. If you had class basketball, you wouldn't have to worry about the Hoosier Dome. You could hold it in Butler Fieldhouse or at New Castle.

"I know the other argument. You would have more state champions, give more kids a chance to excel. The lure and the mystique of being the state champion over all classes would not be there. The smaller schools think that Milan did it in '54, so we can do it this year. I don't think it's any more difficult to compete now than it would have been then. We were blessed with an outstanding group of talent with a coach who knew what to do with the talent. There were a lot of people in '54 who said a small school couldn't do it."

Bob Engel is more to the point.

"If they go to classes, they'll ruin basketball in Indiana," he says.

Even if another small school did win the state championship, however, it's unlikely that it would compare with Milan's victory over Muncie Central. There were just too many extraordinary circumstances that fit together on that night.

The dilemma that a small school in the nineties will always face, no matter what the circumstances, is that it will be in Milan's long shadow. People will always compare it to Milan, and it will most likely not fare favorably.

"I don't think it would change a great deal for Milan's place in history," says Bob Plump. "If they happened to beat a Marion or a Muncie Central, and they did it with a last-second shot and they held the ball for four minutes in the fourth quarter when they were behind, it will change somewhat. I'm still not exactly sure that it would eliminate Milan from conversation."

There are even those associated with the '54 team who would welcome a new champion, a new Milan so to speak.

"If it did happen, I would share the excitement and try to show those kids that they've accomplished something that's been a long time coming," says Engel. "You see a lot of guys, if their record is broken, they don't put the right foot forward. Hey, if somebody can do it, I'm all for them. I have a different attitude toward that kind of stuff. They sacrifice, work hard, and that's what it's all about. If somebody does it, I'll be right there."

Says Wood, "We've enjoyed it all these years. It would be nice for someone else to have the opportunity to enjoy it."

• • •

Jay McCreary, the outspoken boss at Muncie Central, coached three more seasons at the Bearcat helm after losing to Milan in '54. He left with a short tenure, but impressive credentials.

After losing that thriller to Milan in the '54 state finals, the Bearcats opened the next season with seventeen consecutive victories before a late-season setback at Kokomo. They breezed through the first two rounds of the tournament, then handled Rushville in the opening game of the Indianapolis Semistate. That's when they ran into Crispus Attucks, which boasted a more experienced and mature Oscar Robertson. He scored twenty-five points as the Tigers edged Muncie Central by a 71–70 count. Crispus Attucks won the state title a week later.

So after winning the championships in 1951 and 1952, in the three tournaments from 1953 to 1955 Muncie Central lost to a Final Four team in Richmond and two titlists in Milan and Crispus Attucks. The combined margin? Five points.

For the first time in his Bearcat career, McCreary had a team that struggled in 1956. At one point the Bearcats were just 4–10, a lowly mark given the success of the previous few campaigns. They turned it around in time for the tournament and made it to the Sweet Sixteen before losing to Scottsburg. It probably wouldn't have made any difference, because senior Oscar Robertson and Crispus Attucks were on their way to the state's first undefeated state championship.

McCreary's last season seemed like old times. Muncie Central started the 1956–57 campaign 12–1, stumbled a little, and then closed out at 15–5. The post-season brought another Sweet Sixteen appearance and another loss in the afternoon game, this time to Southport by a 71–54 count.

That's when McCreary left for Louisiana State, where he became an assistant coach. His high school mark with the Bearcats remains one of the best and—along with his record as a player on championship teams at Frankfort and Indiana University—earned him enshrinement in the Indiana Basketball Hall of Fame.

Muncie Central, unlike Milan, survived the fifties. The Bearcats, who have a small exhibit in the National Basketball Hall of Fame in Springfield, Massachusetts, remain a perennial power in Indiana basketball. Since McCreary left, Muncie Central has won fifteen sectionals, twelve regionals, seven semistates, and four more state titles, a record eight in all.

McCreary finished his career 132–34, a winning percentage of almost 80 percent. Take away the "disastrous" 14–12 season in 1956 and he was 118–22, a winning percentage of more than 84 percent. He coached in two state finals and won one championship in compiling an incredible tournament record of 41–5.

But the thing that most people remember McCreary for, and the thing that has dogged him for years, is that loss to Milan in 1954. He talks about it openly, calling it his toughest loss ever.

"I'm surprised it had so much impact," he says. "You're talking about a lot of years. Every year it comes up."

Then his voice gets a little bit louder, like he's standing right next to you instead of miles away on the telephone.

"I still feel the same way as I felt then," he says. "We should have won it."

• • •

New Richmond is about two hours northwest of Milan, about a ten-minute drive north of Interstate 74. It's between nowhere and nobody. It's alone, enclosed by a few family farms, a lot of narrow country roads, and probably some broken dreams. It's picturesque and tranquil, even a little soothing in a world dominated by tall skyscrapers, fast-paced living, and the almighty dollar.

It used to be that the only reason people came to visit this tiny hamlet that serves as home to about 400 people was because they either had lost their way or had a lot of time to kill doing nothing. That was, of course, until New Richmond became Hickory and its people became the most loyal extras in the movie *Hoosiers.*

Maybe the Milan people who complain that their town was rural enough to be used in the movie haven't been to New Richmond. That's the only explanation for their behavior. New Richmond was rural, is rural, and always will be rural. Milan is a metropolis compared to it.

Filmmakers found everything—or the lack of everything—in New Richmond. The business list reads quickly—a bank, a post office, a telephone office, a catalog order store, a convenience store, a bar and grill, a plumbing shop, and two churches. This is the kind of small town John Mellencamp sings about.

But being small paid off for New Richmond. It brought that town a fame and identity that no factory or skyscraper could have matched. It was so small and so rural and so isolated that it was the perfect backdrop as the town in the movie.

In fairness to everyone, filmmakers shot scenes in four other towns—Indianapolis, Nineveh, Knightstown, and Brownsburg—but New Richmond is the one that matters today. Most of the other scenes were inside gymnasiums. New Richmond had its entire town in the film, and many of the residents took several weeks off from their jobs to serve as extras in filming at other sites.

As Milan the town still lives for '54, so does New Richmond the town live for '86 and *Hoosiers.* A small sign hangs under the customary town marker. "Welcome to Hickory," it reads. The post office has "Hickory, Ind." under its regular New Richmond identification. The now-closed restaurant was called the Hickory Tree Cafe.

It was the biggest thing to ever happen to New Richmond. It was the biggest thing that ever will happen.

Depending on how you break down the movie, there were about four scenes filmed in or near New Richmond: the scene early in the movie where Gene Hackman meets Dennis Hopper at the local restaurant, the barbershop scene when the townspeople try to tell Hackman how to coach the team, the scene at the feed store when Hackman gets a dinner invitation to Barbara Hershey's house, and the scene in which Hackman is cutting wood in a field behind his house. In all, the crew spent about six working days in New Richmond.

Hollywood didn't just choose New Richmond; it embraced the place. The public service counter at the post office has a small album of photos. It contains pictures of different townspeople with the stars—Hackman, Hopper, Hershey. It wasn't like a film with Madonna, where bodyguards surround her every move. The photos show Gene Hackman on the sidewalk, just standing there like an average human being, talking with people who have probably never been west of the Mississippi, never mind to Hollywood.

New Richmond remembers those few days each fall with the Hickory Festival, a three-day event that usually draws either one of the stars or some of the people behind the cameras. The tourism council offers t-shirts, key chains, posters, and commemorative plates.

Perhaps the best item is a cookbook, "Recipes of the Stars." It contains the favorite recipes of many New Richmond residents and the people who put together the movie. There's Andy's wild duck from filmwriter Angelo Pizzo, garden stuffed peppers from Hackman, midwestern chili from Hopper, and no-measure quiche Lorraine from Hershey. Even Bobby Plump got in the book, with his version of taco supreme and clam chowder.

The best part of the book, though, is not the recipes. It comes at the end when cast members describe their experience in New Richmond.

From Hackman: "Looking back on my days of shooting 'Hoosiers' in New Richmond . . . will always bring pleasant thoughts to mind."

From Pizzo: "We couldn't have found a better place to shoot the town of Hickory. . . . I wish I could thank every one of the people living in New Richmond for their part in making 'Hoosiers' a success."

From director David Anspaugh: "New Richmond . . . isolated and aesthetic . . . with tree shaded houses and red brick buildings . . . perfect as Hickory. . . . and there was this wonderful feeling, just incredible."

• • •

The future of Milan as a town is foggy at best. And if recent trends continue, the fog likely will get denser before lifting.

Milan needs a quick economic fix, the kind where a big industry comes into town and creates a few hundred new jobs. It's past the point where a new grocery store or a restaurant or a gas station could change the spiral.

The barber, Chester Nichols, thinks hope is just about gone. He saw the boom. He's seen the decline. If his scissors and health hold out, he may even see the bust. When he finally pulls down the shade at his shop for the last time, he will close not just the last barbershop in a town that once boasted four such businesses. He will also close a generation.

The barber complains about the water, about the losing basketball team, about the eighties. But he would never move.

Milan is home, no matter what the nineties may hold. One thing is certain: They will not be like the fifties.

"We've got to get somebody on the town board to turn this town around," says Nichols, leaning back in the chair that has remained vacant for most of the afternoon. "For the last ten or fifteen years, they haven't helped this town a bit."

He's watching his business die, along with the death of the Milan basketball team. Of course, there's no connection, but Nichols talks like there is an inherent link between all of the phenomena in a small town.

"We had six chairs, a bench, three barbers," he says. "There were four barbershops with seven barbers in the town. Now I'm the lone survivor. We're down to one barbershop, and the rest are beauty shops. These young men and boys are going to the beauty shops, and the barbershops are going out of business. You find that in every town. When I get ready to hang it up, what will happen to this barbershop? I don't have any idea. I'll put it up for sale. If somebody wants to come in and start barbering, that's fine. If not . . . "

The next minute, he talks of basketball, of the good times and the bad times. The names have become fuzzy over the years, but he remembers the main points.

"I never missed a game," he says of the old days. "I went to one game in 1991. We played so damn lousy that I didn't go back. That was the first year since 1934 that Milan hadn't won a game all year. Who wants to go watch a loser? I just tell it like it is."

Daren Baker, a lifelong resident who owns the Chevrolet dealership a few blocks south of the barbershop, would probably send the current Indian team to Indianapolis in limousines if they could generate some new magic.

Like almost every other new-car dealer in the country, Baker has seen business decline with recessions, the Japanese automakers, and the shift of business from the town.

But that's not the most important thing to Baker. He still makes a good living. He lives just a few blocks from his dealership, so he can walk to work every day. He can lunch with old friends at the Railroad Inn or the country club. He would probably be sincere in one of those commercials that say "life doesn't get any better than this."

"We have basically the same group of people and it's a family," says Baker. "I don't think it's any worse and I don't think it's any better. It's always going to be the same. If that hadn't happened, we'd still have the same people. We just wouldn't be sitting here talking about that game. It just goes on and on and on."

Marc Combs, the old junior high coach who could start one of those memory schools, lives just a few blocks north of the barbershop. He sits in his antique-cluttered living room with his wife, Eva, and Milan residents Barter and Betty Dobson. They also tell it like it is. Marc was a coach, Eva a fan, Barter a bank president and bus driver, and Betty a school secretary.

For better or worse, they are in Milan for life. They've known no other way in all their years. They are too old to learn new ways. They illustrate the Milan stereotype—friendly, considerate, and caring. They treat the stranger like a relative.

"We're a town of people who know each other and are pulled together as a group," says Combs. "We have a feeling for everybody in the community. There is no form of jealousy at all."

Betty Dobson is one of the most vocal of those who have spent their lives in the town. In a forty-year run as the school secretary, she saw teachers and coaches come and go, move on to better things. She saw businesses hang "closed" signs permanently in their windows. She saw people try—and fail—to recreate the magic of Marvin Wood in '54. She is a sentimentalist, the one who realizes maybe more than anyone else that change, no matter how good or how bad, is inevitable.

"Milan was always like a stepping stone for better things," she said. "After '54, we definitely became a stepping stone for people. Everybody ate, drank, and slept basketball. When there was a game, you were there. In came football, volleyball, other girls' sports. People don't go to basketball games now. All of the little schools have consolidated into bigger schools. When I left, school spirit wasn't there.

"Milan isn't home to people anymore. We have a lot of people in and out, stay a few years then leave. We have not progressed much. We've got more vacant buildings than we have open. A lot of the people who owned the land put a price on it that was not feasible. There were a lot of people that didn't want change. They wanted to hold on to what they had, and they're still holding on to it. If a person has something he doesn't want to sell, you can't make him. It makes you sick. It hurts you.

"There was a day when I knew everybody on my street and everybody in the town of Milan. I can't say that anymore. I hope Milan never goes off the map, but we'll never be like we were, just like there will never be another '54 team. I don't care if they do win, there will never be that feeling."

"I don't think we'll ever die," Dobson says with some sort of finality, "but we'll never be what we were."

• • •

The thing about the '54 Milan players, the thing that really, really stands out, is that they aren't a bunch of graying men talking about the old days over a round of beers. They have become a group of folk heroes in Indiana, people who come into the spotlight at least once a year when the state tournament rolls around.

But they don't live for that spotlight. They don't live for the next big anniversary of their conquest (it will be the fortieth in 1994). They have achieved individual success in the post-championship years, whether it be in business, coaching, marriage, or family.

They are still a team, bonded forever by that one fateful night in 1954. Wood organizes the annual reunions, and every year the stories grow longer and the deeds larger. "We're all All-Americans now," says Cutter. But the main subject matter is no longer basketball. The talk often switches to families and retirement.

The public thinks of Milan and thinks of Bob Plump. The team, Plump included, knows it is still a team. It was a team in the beginning. It will be a team in the end.

"We didn't have a star until the final game was over," says Cutter. "It was just one of those things. All of a sudden, a guy hits a shot. With the type of personality he has, everybody likes him. He has the charisma, the attraction. [But] the five guys on the floor and the five guys on the bench were a unit. We didn't have a go-to guy where you put the ball in his hands and he was it. That's not the way Marv Wood coached."

The unit remains visible at the annual reunions, now held at rotating college campuses in Indiana. Seven of the ten players usually gather for those reunions. Truitt was in Texas until his death, Bill Jordan rarely returns from California, and Ken Wendelman chose long ago not to attend. The rest are present, even if they do tell the same stories over and over and over.

"It's like a family reunion," says White. "At every reunion, there are some people who you haven't seen for a while. There are genuine feelings we have, probably more so now than when we were in high school. Every old person looks back on his childhood fondly. When you have a highlight like that, it tends to make you a little closer. As the days mount up, its meaning gets greater."

Says Cutter, "We look back on the day as a good experience. If we didn't have a good time, we would find a reason not to do it."

At each reunion, as the hair grows grayer and often disappears, that day in Butler Fieldhouse takes on a little more importance. Says Engel, "The night when it was all over, who would have thought that this same thing would still be on the top of the pile? The longer it goes, the more it grows. It's like a Christmas tree and you turn the light on. That's the feeling you get."

New generations will hear the story of Wood and the Indians. The details might become clouded, but the impact will remain unaffected. The Milan dream will always be the dream of every small school in Indiana. If someone else did it, then we can do it.

"I think every small boy or girl who plays basketball in the state of Indiana has a dream of playing on a championship team," says Wood. "A lot dream only about the county championship or the conference championship. They would all love to dream of the state championship, but a lot think that is the impossible dream."

The biggest problem most of these players have today is not dealing with their legendary status but coming to grips with their impending mortality. They still find it hard to believe that Ron Truitt is gone, a victim of cancer. They still find it hard to believe that Marvin Wood, the coach, has the same disease.

They want to hang on, but everyone knows it will end someday. Says Plump, "Everybody knows, deep down, that we're going to lose some members. You don't know when you're going to pick up the paper and somebody is going to be dead."

The reunions will still occur, probably until just two players remain. The same stories will be told.

"I think the big thing will be what happens to Woody," says Cutter. "I hope he beats this thing. He will be a competitor. If something happens to Woody, we'll still get together but it will be different. At the time, he was our coach. Today, he's our friend. There's a difference. We still have the respect for him, but he's become more than a coach now."

Says White, "We're on a downhill slide now. A few will disappear in the next ten years. We'll just slide into oblivion. Time takes care of everything."

But they will leave behind an enduring legacy, one of dignity, courage, and an incredible will to win against the most outstanding of odds. Theirs is a story for the ages.

"Fifty years from now, it will still be legendary," says Schroder.

And even that may be a modest estimate.

GREG GUFFEY, a 1991 graduate of the
University of Notre Dame, is the author of *More
Than a Game: A History of Boys' Basketball in Henry
County* and assistant director of communications
in the Indiana House of Representatives.

BOB HAMMEL is Sports Editor for the *Herald-
Times* in Bloomington.